Forest in the Life of the Khasis

About the Author

Dr. Rekha M. Shangpliang *did her M.A. in Sociology* from North-Eastern Hill University Shillong, and attained 1st Class 1st position (Gold Medalist). Thereafter she completed *her M.Phil and Ph.D. from* North-Eastern Hill University, Shillong. She was a Lecturer in Sociology at St. Edmund's College, Shillong and presently a *senior Lecturer at the Department of Sociology*, North Eastern Hill University, Shillong. She has contributed many articles in various academic journals and edited volumes.

Forest in the Life of the Khasis

Rekha M. Shangpliang
Department of Sociology
North Eastern Hill University
Shillong

CONCEPT PUBLISHING COMPANY PVT. LTD.
NEW DELHI-110059

ISBN-13-978-81-8069-667-1

First Published 2010

Published and Printed by

Concept Publishing Company Pvt. Ltd.
Regd. Office:
A/15-16, Commercial Block, Mohan Garden
New Delhi-110059 (India)
Phones : 25351460, 25351794, *Fax* : 091-11-25357109
Email : publishing@conceptpub.com
Website: www.conceptpub.com

Editorial Office:
H-13, Bali Nagar, New Delhi-110 015, India.

Cataloging in Publication Data-- *Courtesy:* D.K. Agencies (P) Ltd. <docinfo@dkagencies.com>

Shangpliang, Rekha M.
Forest in the life of the Khasis / Rekha M. Shangpliang.
p. cm.
Originally presented as the author's thesis (Ph. D.)--North Eastern Hill University.
Includes bibliographical references (p.).
Includes index.
ISBN 13: 9788180696671

1. Community forests--India--United Khāsi-Jaintia Hills. 2. Forest ecology--India--United Khāsi-Jaintia Hills. 3. Khasi (Indic people)--Social life and customs. 4. Khasi (Indic people)--Economic conditions. 5. Human ecology--India--United Khāsi-Jaintia Hills. 6. Forests and forestry--Social aspects--India--United Khāsi-Jaintia Hills. 7. Forests and forestry--Economic aspects--India--United Khāsi-Jaintia Hills. I. Title.

DDC 337.750899593 22

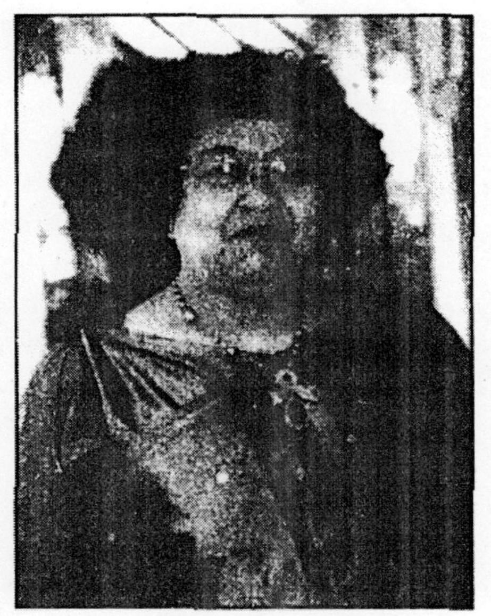

Dedicated

To

My mother

Mrs. Sidona Shangpliang

who taught me to appreciate
the beauty of nature

"Sa shisien pat kin win ki khlaw
Sa shisien pat kin khih ki maw,
Kum kiwei pat ki sngi kin mih,
Da kumwei pat ka ri kan ih
Lada ngi don ki shkor ban sngew
Aiu ka kren ka Mei-Ramew"

"Once again the trees will sound
Once again the rocks will move
Like in the past the days will come
In another way the land will mature
If we have ears to listen
To what Mother Earth has to say........"

Soso Tham " Ka Meirilung "

PREFACE

This book is an outgrowth of my Ph.D. thesis under the title "Forest in the Life of the Khasis : A Study in the Role of Forest in Khasi Socio-economic Structure" which I have worked on for almost 6 years. The idea of bringing out this book sparked off from a casual tea-time conversation that I had with my friends and colleagues at the department who held out high opinion about the relevance of the work to the present ecological scenario of the state and about its usefulness for educating and generating eco-consciousness among the people. It also occurred to me that besides being useful to general readers, this book if made available, would be beneficial for academicians, planners and research scholars as well. Keeping this in mind, I set to pattern out my work into two separate volumes. The present volume is based on the ecological dimensions of forest in Khasi culture. It is intended to disseminate knowledge about Khasis, their land, ecology and economy and the parameters of forest usage among the Khasis. While the other volume is meant for a deeper understanding about the Khasi concept of forest and ecology; their implications in the socio-economic and spiritual life of the Khasis including a case study of two sample villages with empirical data-base.

This Book is divided into 4 chapters. First chapter lays emphasis on the background of Khasi society throwing light on the origin, history and ecological heritage of the Khasi people. This chapter also discusses at length the system of classification of land and forest in Khasi Hills, the land tenure system and forest cover information of the State.

The second chapter focuses on the Khasi concept of forest explaining the various connotations of forest as a sacred entity which finds expression in Khasi beliefs, legends, folklores, folktales and literature. With a view to analyse the eco-theandric view of nature, this chapter discovers the wholeness of nature and ecology in the socio-religious life of the Khasis, reminiscent to those found in the life of the Maler tribe studied by L.P. Vidyarthi.

Chapter 3 gives a detailed account of the parameters of forest usage in Khasi society covering various aspects of Khasi life and culture such as shelter, food, medicinal herbs, musical instruments, weaving and dying, rituals and ceremonies.

Chapter 4 is a conclusive evidence of the fact that nature still occupies a central place in Khasi life and culture in spite of large scale destruction of forest by some vested interests to satisfy his needs and greed. Truely, today it is quite a deplorable sight to see our forests disappearing at an alarming rate, but this state of things has come to the fore only in recent times. In the past, the Khasis adored nature and treated her with due respect and reverence. While it is true that we cannot get back the golden era or "Aiom Ksiar" when men and nature and beasts lived peacefully, there is still a ray of hope that the tradition of eco-spirituality embedded in Khasi culture can serve as a starting point to continue the pristine relationship with the forest that has existed in the past.

The weaknesses of this book are precisely my own—its strengths mine, too. There were several people who extended invaluable help, which I am eager to recognize here. I sincerely thank the faculty at the Department of Sociology, NEHU, who have supported me throughout my years as a student and even today as a colleague. A special word of thanks to Prof. A.C. Sinha an erudite mentor in the early stages of my work and still a valued supporter in every way. To others who read all portions of my manuscript and provided advice and criticism, I am indebted to all of them.

The most important acknowledgement, however, is reserved for my father. His support and good judgment is recorded at every page.

Last but not the least, I dedicate this book to my most beloved mother who passed away five months before the book was due to be out. I'm sure she would have been very proud of me as she always dreamed of her youngest daughter achieving new heights in her life and career.

Rekha M. Shangpliang
Department of Sociology
NEHU, Shillong

CONTENTS

GLOSSARY OF VERNACULAR TERMS

Bylla Sngi	- daily labourer
Bylla Surok	- Muster roll
Ka Kper	- Homestead Land
Ka iiuh moi	- a harrow
Ka Latar	- A type of tree, the bark of which is used as ropes for constructing houses
Ka Rashi	- a sickle
Kha	- born of
Khanatang bad Puriskam	- Khasi folktales and legends
Khlam	- Serious plague
Khlaw Shimet	- Private Forest
Khlaw Shnong	- Village Forest
Khnam	- Khasi arrow
Khoh	- Bamboo basket
Ki khlaw ki btap	- the forest
Ki Lum Makachiang	- the Himalayas
Knup	- Bamboo Umbrella, Rain shields
Kwai	- Betelnut
Kynbat Samthiah	- a particular flower the petals of which open when the sun rises and close as the sun begins to set
Dawai Kynbat	- Khasi Folk Medicine
Dieng Kseh Bilat	- Pure Oak
Durbar Shnong	- Village council where all disputes are settled
Haat	- weekly market
Hynniewtrep-Hynniewskum	- Seven Huts – Seven Nests
Ja	- Cooked Rice
Law Adong or Law Shnong	- Protected or village forest

Law Kyntang	-	Sacred Groves
Law Sumar	-	Private Forest
Lei Khlaw	-	Forest spirits
Lei Lum	-	mountain or hill spirits
Lei Muluk	-	God of the State
Lei Umtong	-	Water Spirits
Lei wah	-	river Spirits
Lyngknot	-	Wooden stool for sitting upon
Mawshamok	-	White Stones
Meiramew	-	Mother Earth
Mohkhiew	-	Khasi Hoe
Myntris	-	ministers
Niam	-	religion
Nuli, Pantaro, Sohtung	-	Species of trees used as a dye
Poikha poiman	-	marriage
Putharo Pukhlein	-	Rice Pancakes
Pynthor	-	Plains or wet paddy
Ri-Kynti	-	Private Land
Ri Lum	-	Hilly Land
Ri-Raid	-	Community Land
Rngai	-	Shadow or spirit of the dead
Sapied Siej	-	Sharp Edged Bamboo Stick
Sboh sem masi	-	lumps of decomposed cowdung
Sboh Sem sniang	-	Pig Sty
Shang Kwai	-	Bamboo Basket for storing betelnut
Shoh Kba	-	thrashing of sheaves
Shoh Maw	-	stone crusher
Shylliah	-	Mats made of plaited cane
Siej lieh	-	species of bamboo out of which mats are woven
Sohpetbneng	-	the navel of Heaven
Tang Jait	-	a ceremony by which a new clan bearing the name of the non-Khasi mother is created
Tari	-	kitchen knife

Thang Shyrti	- Jhum Cultivation
Thup or Thak	- a Stake of firewood
Tiew Diengsong	- a particular flower associated with the onset of fever
Tih Shyiap	- sand tiller
Tymmen Shnong	- Village headman
U Blei nongbuh nongthaw	- God the Supreme Being
U ryngkew U basa	- the guardian spirit
U Sdie	- An axe for felling trees and shrubs
Wait Bnoh	- hooked knife
Wait Lyngkut	- curved knife
Wait Sum	- butcher's knife

NB: The alphabetical order here follows the Khasi alphabets.

INTRODUCTION

The Khasis are one of the tribal communities of the North East who have maintained a very close symbiotic relationship with the environment since time immemorial, and whose ethno-cultural traits have been greatly influenced by the natural surroundings. Like any other tribal group, the Khasis have a very close affinity to nature therefore forest which is an important component of nature is intricately linked to the life of the Khasis.

For a Khasi the forest is a well-loved home, a game sanctuary and also an abode of worship, all rolled in one, around which his social, cultural and religious activities revolve.

In the words of H.O Mawrie

"*U Khasi U im bad ka mariang, bad ka mariang ka im bad U*", which literally means: "A Khasi lives with nature and nature lives with him". This strong bond created between the Khasi and the environment also leads one to believe that the forest, which is a vital component of the environment, is the very source of life. It is in the Khasi custom to believe that the earth with all its bounty is referred to as *Meiramew* which means "*mother earth*", *Meiramew* being a combination of land, forest, rivers and streams, the Khasis do not separate these elements of the mother and the earth as separate entities. Forests are a treasure trove of a large variety of food. It is estimated that 60-70 per cent of the food consumed by the tribals comes from the forest. It is a familiar sight to see Khasi women and children setting off into the woods to collect edible fruits and roots. They look upon the forest as the ultimate storehouse of wealth, a source of immediate help at difficult times, a readymade kitchen and a

Khasi would spare no pains from running to the forest and grabbing any edible fruit to offer to an unexpected guest who just pays a sudden visit.

Forest products such as tubers, rhizome, succulent shoots, fruits and mushrooms have provided the villagers with an alternative source of economic activity besides supplementing their basic requirements of food. An estimated study reveals that most of the village folk who still continue the collection of wild mushroom from the Upper Shillong Reserve Forest in Laitkor peak collects about 5 kgs. of mushroom per day and sell them in the markets of Shillong. An interesting study made by a well known Khasi author, S. Khongsit brings out a list of 113 food items comprising edible leaves, bark of trees, fruits and vegetables that are procured from the forest which begin with the prefix "*Ja*", which in Khasi means 'cooked rice'.

With the increase in the realization of global value of medicinal plants, today the medicinal plant trade (eco-piracy) is a hidden economy. According to a research conducted by the North Eastern Bio-diversity Research Cell, the North Eastern Region alone has more than 10,278 plant species documented so far and contributes to more than 17 per cent of the country's genetic resources. Besides, the herbal practitioners conducted a preliminary survey covering 200 herbal practitioners on the use of medicinal plants and related activities in East Khasi Hills, Jaintia Hills and West Khasi Hills and Ri Bhoi, which documented the use of more than 150 species of plants. There is a growing concern among the local practitioners and environmentally conscious citizens for the rapid rate of species depletion in certain areas due to the absence of any effective regulatory and monitoring agency. There is a lurking danger of biopiracy, which may be responsible for the unrestricted depletion of the State's bio-resources. However for any research along the field of forest as a source of medicinal plants it is necessary to reflect on its traditional assumption and then to analyze the Indigenous Knowledge System (IKS) pertaining to their usage in the Khasi society.

Forest has provided the Khasi with food, fodder, water, shelter and medicine. For their food, they collect from forest a great variety of minor forest produce. The forests of Khasi Hills possess a vast resource of medicinal plants and herbs on which the Khasis have traditionally depended for the treatment of various diseases. The rural folk have practiced this age-old herbal-lore and developed the system of Khasi folk medicine (*dawai kynbat*) into a lasting tradition, which continues even today.

Thus the Khasi have a very close affinity with the forests, which encompasses a wide spectrum of life including food, medicine, shelter, housing, agricultural implements, musical instruments besides having a strong cultural link.

Like many other hill people of the North East, the economy of the Khasi is essentially land and forest oriented. Agriculture is the mainstay of the people, which is largely carried out, in primitive method of *jhum* or shifting cultivation. This practice is, however, considered destructive as vast areas of forest is cleared and burnt so that cultivation can be carried on for at least 3 to 4 consecutive years. After a gap of 4 to 5 years, those areas are again used for cultivation without allowing the land to rejuvenate. *Jhum* cultivation, which is locally known as "*thang shyrti*" is still practiced by a large section of the community in Khasi Hills.

Nature has endowed the Khasi homeland with the quality of soil and climate suitable for a wide variety of crops, fruits and vegetables. The Central plateau of the district is suitable for growing high altitude paddy, maize, millets, potato and temperate fruits and vegetables; while the southern slopes bordering Bangladesh grows plantation crops like oranges, bananas, pineapples, erecanuts, betel leaves, bay leaf etc. In the northern side of the district bordering Assam, paddy, maize, banana, and pineapple are widely grown. But the Khasi economy has essentially remained a tribal economy till today, characterized by simple technology and primitive method, geographical isolation and single-family unit of production and consumption. No appreciable change appears to have taken place in the style and technique of rural economy despite Government efforts during the last 50 years and more of planning for development.

A majority of the village industries in the Khasi Hills are forest based. Industries like carpentry, cane and bamboo work, bee-keeping, broomstick making etc. derive their raw materials from the forest which provides employment opportunities to a large section of the rural people who work in the forests by felling trees and sawing timbers in lime kilns and burning and selling charcoal. The womenfolk and children of the poor families traditionally eke out their living by cutting and selling firewood, collecting broomstick, selling wild fruits and vegetables while the men folk penetrate deeper into the forest and gather valuable orchids and wild flora for earning handsome prices for the urban rich.

Thus forest occupies the central place in the socio-economic and religious life of the Khasi who constitute an integral component of the forest ecosystem. The forest has always been a plus item and it will continue to remain so with added interest and it will be on forestry that the future economy of our people can find sound footing (Mathew, 1980:26).

A Word on the Existing Literature

Literature has little to offer on environmental issues in Meghalaya in general and the Khasi Hills in particular. Some scholarly works of research has already been done on subjects relating to the forest resources of Meghalaya, the existence of Sacred Groves, the natural environment of the Khasis and System of Forest Management in the Khasi Hills etc. However, the vagueness of such references and the obvious richness of the subject led to the initiation of this present study. A few books that contained references relevant to the present study are :

A.C Sinha's book *Beyond the Trees, Tigers and Tribes* (1993) which has thrown light on the system of Forest administration starting from the colonial to post-colonial stage with particular reference to early efforts of forest utilization in North East frontier. His work reveals some alarming facts about the discovery of valuable plant species in and around the forests of Khasi and Jaintia Hills. David Arnold and Ramachandra Guha's co-edited book *Nature, Culture Imperialism* (1996), introduces the reader to the nature-man relationship embedded in the cultures of South East Asia. H.O Mawrie's book *The Khasi Milieu* (1981) is a compilation of some important themes in Khasi life and culture like marriage, family, religion, village, administration, folktales etc. and he devotes 2 chapters exclusively to the role of nature in Khasi life. His resounding declaration "A Khasi lives with nature and nature lives in him" summarises the close affinity between the Khasi and nature. Mawrie also relates the symbolic significance of trees by associating them with Khasi folk tales and legends. Mawrie's book also unfolds the rich storehouse of Khasi folk tales and legends that centre on things and objects seen in nature. Besides the moral values attached to these folk tales, they are also an important source of information about the long attachment between the Khasi and nature that have existed since time immemorial. The book *"The Last Frontier-People and Forests in Mizoram"*(1996) written by Daman Singh presents a 'realistic' account of Mizoram backed by some useful data on forest as a mode of resource use. The author interprets the term "forest" in Mizoram in two ways: forest cover which includes the total area under tree or bamboo vegetation and forest by use which excludes those areas used for non-forestry purposes, e.g. *jhumming*. With regard to *jhum* cultivation, it is the well-established Mizo custom of '*tlawmngaihna*' which goes along with the principle of collective use of land for shifting cultivation. Daman Singh notes the strong element of mutual cooperation shared by members of the Mizo community in agricultural operations. She also examines the changing interaction of man and his environment in Mizoram over the span of a century and attributes this change to a set of four parameters: Belief Systems, Domain, Social institutions and Technology.

A number of books in vernacular literature also proved

fruitful for the present study. Amongst them, K. Dhirendro Ramsiej (1992) in his book entitled "*Ka Mariang ha U Khasi bad Ki purinam-puriskam*", brings out the intricate relationship between nature and culture amongst the Khasis. A number of Khasi folktales and legends associated with nature-man relationship have been highlighted by the author which throws light on the part played by nature in shaping the Khasi culture. In the book, "*Ka Dieng bad ka Culture Jong Ngi*", S. Khongsit narrates the numerous species of trees, plant and herbs that grow in Khasi-Jaintia hills which have played an important role in the life of the Khasi both in the past and present. Talking about the role of theology and culture in the maturity of human civilization, H.O. Mawrie in his book "*Ka Theology Jong ka Niam Khasi*" stresses the importance of understanding the theology of a tribe. The author also speaks about the role played by the environment in shaping the theology and belief of humanity. Man is already a part of nature and nature is already a part of man.

Published literature in the form of official reports and documents has also been useful sources of information on historical and administrative matters. On the whole, what proved to be most fruitful was the real life situations revealed by my field trips which formed part of my research work for my Ph. D. These visits aimed at gaining insight through interview and observation on the role and importance of forest in the life of the Khasis.

1 THE KHASIS-PEOPLE, LAND AND ECOLOGY

The People

The Khasis occupy a unique position both from ethnic and linguistic points of view among the congeries of the tribes inhabiting the mountainous terrain of India's North East. There are numerous interpretations of the word "Khasi". Hamlet Bareh suggests that the term "*Khasi*" means "*born of the mother*"; "*kha*" means "*born of*" and "*si*" refers to "*ancient mother*", thus bringing out the matrilineal character of the Khasis who trace their descent from the mother. The origin of the Khasis as a race is shrouded in mystery, which has led historians to trace the roots of history in order to understand, "who is a Khasi?"[1]

The Land Reforms Commission for Khasi Hills (Vol. 1) opined that a person who is acceptable as a Khasi is one whose parents descended since time immemorial from the descendants of the people inhabiting *Ka Ri Khadar Doloi*, *Ka Ri Laiphew Syiem*, or who has adopted Khasi socio-political customs and way of life, conducts and comports himself as a Khasi, speaks Khasi language, follows a matrilineal system, and in the case of male adults have a right to take part in traditional durbars of the Khasis in a place where he lives or do take part in the election of hereditary Chiefs of his *elaka* where popular election is held in which women cannot take part and is accepted by the rest of the people as belonging to their tribe [R.T. Rymbai and others, *Report of Land Reforms Commission for Khasi Hills* (Vol. I), Shillong, 1973, p.34, Government of Meghalaya].

David Roy defined a Khasi as a person who is a descendant of the folk, who found a home in these hills and is governed by Khasi laws of consanguinity and kinship. A Khasi is a Khasi because of his religion (*Niam*) which regulates all his thoughts and activities.

Hamlet Bareh describes "Khasi" as a general term encompassing the various tribes and sub-tribes inhabiting the Khasi and Jaintia Hills, namely :

1. *Khynriams* or *Nonglum* (Khasi proper) inhabiting the middle ranges of the Khasi Hills, comprising the *Khynriams* proper and their allied tribes in the central plateau;
2. The *Pnars* inhabiting the central plateau of the Jaintia Hills. The *Pnars* are also called the *Syntengs*, but they prefer to be called *Pnars*;
3. The *War* people of the south, comprising the *Shella* people and their allied tribes;
4. The *Amwi* people and their allied war, *Synteng* and other tribes in the south Jaintia Hills who form apparent tribe of the present *Khasi-Pnars* in their earliest period of settlement in the land;
5. The *Bhoi* people, both *Khasi* and *Pnar* inhabiting the north of Khasi and Jaintia Hills with their different sub-groups.[2]

According to A.S. Khongphai, the non-controversial definition of a Khasi is a person born of a Khasi mother, irrespective of the fact whether he is a Khasi or a non-Khasi. However, their definition has been modified with the introduction of Khasi Lineage Bill, 1997, which defines a Khasi as one whose parents are/were both Khasis and whose clan name is taken from the mother. For those born of a Khasi father and a non-Khasi mother, the Bill has invoked the old custom of "*Tang Jait*" a ceremony by which a new clan bearing the name of the non-Khasi mother is created. The Bill further states that to be a Khasi the person will have to know the Khasi language unless prevented from knowing it by circumstances beyond his control like living outside the area. He must also observe and be governed by the Khasi matrilineal system, Khasi law of inheritance and succession and the Khasi laws of consanguinity and kinship.

In short, as mentioned by Mr. Thomas, the Magistrate of the District Council Court, to be a Khasi, one has to live like a Khasi, dress like a Khasi, eat like a Khasi, speak Khasi language and follow the Khasi customs and traditions. Though all Khasis have fundamentally the same language and social structure, their culture, dialects, economy, social usage and political organisation vary greatly owing to the ecological and politico-historical differences among them.

The various myths and legends associated with the origin of the Khasis provide us with ample evidence about their long period of association with Gods and heavenly beings. One such interpretation is incorporated in their legend of the *Hynniewtrep-Hynniewskum* or the Seven Huts—the Seven Nests. This legend tells the story of how God in the beginning created sixteen families and let them stay with him in heaven. He allowed them to move freely between Heaven and Earth with the help of a golden ladder which touched the top of a mountain peak name *Sohpetbneng* (The Navel of Heaven) until one day when seven of them chose to remain on earth leaving the remaining nine in heaven. From that day God removed the ladder and the seven families on earth came to be known as *Ki Hynniew Ha Tbian* (The Seven Below) and those who remained in Heaven as *Ki Khyndai Hajrong* (The Nine Above). The Khasis, as we know them today, according to their timeless tale are the descendants of the Seven Below, and they have flourished throughout their beautiful land.

The migration pattern of the Khasis has also led to a paucity of beliefs and traditions about the movement of this tribe into the hills that took place in times long past. The commonly accepted view is that they came from the far East and used the same route of migration followed by other immigrants from Burma. Gurdon states that many affinities can be traced between the Khasis and the Mon-Khmer from the Far East on grounds of resemblance.[3] It is also interesting to note that the Himalayan ranges have a close association with the Khasis because they have their own name for these ranges '*Ki Lum Makachiang*' which indicates that the Khasis had once settled in the neighbourhood of the Himalayas, or at the foothills of these mountains around Darrang, Sadiya and Dibrugarh.[4]

According to J.R. Logan, the Khasis have a close relationship with the Mons or Talaings of Pegu and Tenasserim, the Khmers of Combodia and the inhabitants of Aman. Logan identifies a tribe called the Palungs who inhabit the Shan state of Myanmar, as the closest kinsmen of the Khasis. In the opinion of Roy, the Khasis belong to the Mongoloid family on account of the similarity of the languages of these two groups, stating that the close similarity between the Mundas and Khasis rites and rituals during veneration of the dead. Walter G. Griffith was of the opinion that the Mundas who are located in the Chotanagpur area were the ancestors of the Khasis.

While it is true that the Khasis have established themselves in these hills for a very long time and that the process of negation was from east to west, many support the view that the Khasis are linguistically and racially an offshoot of the Monkhmer branch of the Austro-Asiatic stock and are believed to be due remnants of the first Mongolian overflow into India.[5]

Land and Geography

The Khasi Hills are located in the northeastern corner of India in the middle of the Meghalaya plateau with East and West Garo Hills lying towards its West and Karbi Anglong District of Assam towards the East.

The United Khasi and Jaintia Hills was one of the districts in the erstwhile composite state of Assam. After the creation of the Autonomous State of Meghalaya on 2nd April 1970 and the attainment of full statehood on 21st January 1972, the United Khasi and Jaintia Hills and the Garo Hills District formed the constituent Districts of Meghalaya with the headquarters at Shillong and Tura respectively. Thereafter, the Khasi Hills District was divided into two districts, namely the East Khasi Hills District and the West Khasi Hills District on 28th October 1976. However, on June 4th 1992, East Khasi Hills District was further divided into two administrative districts of East Khasi Hills District and Ri Bhoi District. According to the Census of India 2001, the total population of East and West Khasi Hills is 955,109 persons.

Climate

In association with the varying physiography, the climate ranges from temperate to tropical with sufficient supply of rainfall that helps the growth of luxuriant and thick vegetation. The orography of the southern part of Meghalaya too helps the occurrence of heavy monsoon rain where Mawsynram and Cherrapunjee receives the highest annual rainfall in the world (Sarma, 2003). The winter season begins in December and continues till the end of February with the temperature falling down to 1°C in some high altitude areas. The lives of the inhabitants here are thus to a large extent ruled by the decree of nature. The climate is pleasant in autumn and spring and it is suitable for various crops and fruits. With the varying climate and sufficient rainfall, evergreen tropical forests are to be found on the northern slopes.

Minerals

Mineral deposits in the Khasi Hills have acquired a unique place in the geographical map of the country. The principal mineral deposits being limestone and coal. Uranium deposits in Domïasiat area of West Khasi Hills District is one of the 12th largest deposits in the world.[6]

Mountain and River System

Due to the undulating topography, one finds the principal rivers of the region running from the higher ranges with their tributaries flowing into the Brahmaputra river. These rivers situated in the region of heavy rainfall are seasonally fed by the monsoon rains. The principal rivers that flow towards the north are *the Khri, the Umtrew, the Wah Umïam* and *the Wah Umkhen* and those which flow towards the south are *the Kynshi iong, the Umïew* or *Umïam Mawphlang* and *the Umngot*. Most of these rivers are swift-flowing because of the rapid change in height and rocky land which carves its pathway into deep gorges thereby forming magnificent waterfalls and cataracts. Some of these well known majestic waterfalls are *Kshaid Noh-Sngi-Thiang, Kshaid Noh-Ka-Likai, Kshaid Dain-Thlen, Kshaid Umshyrpi* or Beadon Falls, *Kshaid Sunapani* or Bishop's Falls, *Kshaid Umdiengpun* or Elephants Falls, *Kshaid Weitdem* or Sweet Falls (*Kshaid* is the Khasi term for waterfall).

Flora and Fauna

Perhaps the floristic composition of the Khasi Hills is nowhere commented with such appreciation as has been done by Dr. Joseph Dalton Hooker in his Himalayan Journals. Hooker's journey up to these hills in 1850 was indeed rewarding, taking into account his valuable observations of the richness and variety of the colour, form and size of each blossoming plant. In his own words, "It is extremely difficult to give within the limits of this narrative any idea of the Khasi flora which is, in extent and number of fine plants, the richest in India, and probably in all Asia, the collected upwards of 2,000 flowering plants within ten miles of the station of Churra (Cherra) besides 150 ferns, with a profusion of masses, lichen and fungi......... Orchidaceae are, perhaps, the largest natural order in the Khasia where fully 250 kinds grow, chiefly on trees and rocks, but many are terrestrial, inhabiting damp woods and grassy slopes. I doubt whether in any other part of the globe the species of orchids outnumber those of any other natural order, or form so large a population of the flora."

On the whole, there can still be ample scope for exploration of plant species in these hills. However, one cannot deny the Herculean efforts of plant explorers like Griffith (1847), Hooker (1854), Clarke (1889), Bor (1938, 1942), Biswas (1941, 1943), Kingdon-Ward (1960) and Burhill (1965) who have given accounts of the flora of this region. The first systematic treatment of the flora of the north eastern region is by Kanjilat *et al.* (1939-40), a work in five volumes (incomplete). The first four volumes cover the Dicotyledons, chiefly the woody species being forest flora and the fifth volume by Bor (1940) deals with the Germinae only.

The establishment of the Botanical Survey of India in the country way back in 1890 led to some significant efforts to create public interest in the plant life of Khasi Hills after 1956. One laudible effort of the BSI has been to work in collaboration with the North Eastern Council in launching a programme for the cultivation, multiplication, preservation and supply of orchids to collectors at a cheaper rate with a view to prevent depletion of the natural habitats.

A careful survey of the vegetation in these hills reveals some alarming facts and remarkable instances of disjunct distribution. The discovery of novelties of very rare species have been found such as *Nymphaea pygmea* (South Siberia and North China); *Magnolia lanugimosa* (Nepal); *Hemalium schleichii* (Burma), etc. which add to the diversity of species composition in the region.

Another remarkable feature of the floristic variety of the Khasi Hills is found in the Sacred Groves located at several areas in and around Shillong Peak, Mawphlang and Mawsmai. These groves are home to some very rare species of orchids and a number of plants. A number of botanical explorations over the last 50 years have revealed that *Ilex khasiana* a small evergreen tree that grows with thick foliage in the forests of Meghalaya is facing extinction.

The National Orchidarium at Shillong maintains over 300 species of orchids of North Eastern Region and the Experimental Garden at Umiam (Barapani) maintains the germplasm bank of many rare and threatened orchids, besides several rare, endangered, medicinal plants (Mao *et al.*, 1999).

A recent survey conducted by the National Botanical Research Institute, Lucknow which is one of the premier institutes of Council of Scientific and Industrial Research (CSIR) has undertaken a project on research and development work in the North Eastern Region. Under this project, Dr. V. P. Kapoor, Head of the Plant Chemistry Division, National Botanical Research Institute reported that Meghalaya has enough dye–yielding plants which may be utilised to set up local dye producing units. It was reported that the roots and stem of a prominent plant *Rubia cordifolia* (local name Sacre) contain yellow dye and the leaves of *Camellia caduca* (Samkhi) contain brown dye. With the increasing trend now-a-days for use of textile and consumer goods dye by natural dyes, there is enough potential to use these dye yielding plants for local industry and generate awareness to local people and entrepreneurs through training programmes.[7]

Fauna

"The fauna of the Khasi Hills is intimately connected with the geomorphological evolution of the area. This region served as a fauna gateway through which their Indo-Chinese elements of Oriental fauna and Palaearctic montane fauna spread to the main subcontinent. As a result, a complex assemblage of Indo-Chinese Indo-Myanmar, Ethiopian and Palaearctic montane elements could now be observed" (Dr. C. Radhakrishnan, Zoologist and Officer-in-Charge, E. Regional Station, Zoological Survey of India).

The existing eco-systems are conducive to the growth of evergreen forests that are the habitat of rich mammalian fauna and other forms of animal life, mammals like the Hoolock (Gibbon) the Golden Cat (*Felis termnuckii* Vigors and Horefeld) the leopard cat (*Felis bangalensis* Kerr), the Jungle Cat (*Felis chaus* Guldenstaedt), to name a few have added a unique assemblage to the oriental fauna of the Khasi Hills.

Besides mammals, birds of various species are found in abundance in the forests specially in low altitude areas like the forests of the Nongpoh-Lailad areas in Khasi Hills. The common birds found include the long tailed Broadbill (*Psarosomus dalhousiae* Jameson), the Burmese Roller (*Coradias bengalensis affinis* Horsfeld), the Blue throated Barbet (*Megalaima asiatica* Latham), the Red-vented Bulbul (*Pynonotus cafer bengalensis* Blyth), the Himalayan Black Bulbul (*Hypsipetes madagascariensis psaroides vigors*), the Hill Mynah (*Gracula religiosa* Linn) etc. which are only a few of the many exotic species of birds found. Reptiles and fish species of the Khasi Hills also exhibit excellent qualities of adaptation to the climate and topography of the region. Mention should be made about the exotic species of butterflies like the Blue Peacock, the orange oak leaf and the Bhutan Glory that add to the interesting assemblage of insects in the region.

According to official reports on the faunal resources in the seven sister states of the North East, 650 species of plants and 70 species of animals who find a habitat in the region have been listed as endangered due to human depredation, poaching and other non-planned and non-forestry activities.[8] While there is a concerted effort to preserve the fragile eco-system in the region which has been identified as one of the 18 'hot spot' areas in the world with reference to threats to the rich bio-diversity. What is of serious concern today is the fact that there is a lack of positive activity on the part of both the Central and State Governments which has given little scope about the knowledge of the extent of bio-diversity, of micro-organisms, particularly of bacteria and viruses. Among the North Eastern States, Meghalaya is considered to have faunal diversity and vegetation including forest cover that is diverse in its climatic season which shows the richest assemblage of eco-diversity. The State recorded a total of 5538 species of faunal wealth in the country.[9]

CLASSIFICATION OF LAND AND FOREST IN KHASI HILLS

'Land' and 'Forest' are both the natural endowments of nature on humankind. They have both played a historical role in the social, economic and cultural life of human communities through the centuries and one cannot undermine the importance of land and forest both as a resource and as property. As a valuable natural resource, land and forest represent the principal forms of wealth, are a symbol of social status and a constant source of economic and political power. Thus, ownership of these two vital resources has often led to a distinct control over positions of prestige, affluence and power in societies around the world. Land and Forest being an integral part of human habitat has since time immemorial led to a wide variation in the pattern of rights over them. In the cognitive frame, there is no ambiguity about people's rights over these two valuable resources, nor is there any similarity in the system of management of these two natural productive resources.[10] The concept of 'Land' and 'Forest' have in recent years evoked an equivocal response which makes it pertinent for us to discuss them as separate entities.

LAND TENURE SYSTEM IN THE KHASI HILLS

Land locally known as "*Ri*" by the Khasis has a deep attachment to their pattern of social organization and permeates every aspect of their socio-economic life. Land to the Khasis is a "gift of nature" that belongs to the community, therefore access to land not ensures economic security for the individual, but control over it symbolizes territorial integrity for the community as a whole.[11] Realizing the need to determine who may be recognized and accepted as a Khasi, the Land Reforms Commission for Khasi Hills, 1975 stated that the social customs, religious beliefs and the singular pattern of inheritance prevalent among the Khasis are among the predominant factors of the people.[12] In the opinion of the Commission, the dominant factor in determining as to who is a Khasi, is one's adherence to the matrilineal system of inheritance, observance of the socio-political system and acceptance by the Khasi Community as one who belongs to it. Land for a Khasi is thus a prized possession of economic gains as much as a sign of economic prosperity with a deep emotional attachment.

The Khasi principalities have been known by the common expression that has been handed down by oral tradition extending upto the present day as "*Ka Ri Khadar Doloi*", "*Ka Ri Laiphew Syiem*", which literally means the land of 12 *Dolois*, the land of 30 *syiems*. The *Dolois* were 'chieftains' under the raja of Jaintiapur and Syiems were rajahs in the Khasi Hills[13] while there are no official records to verify the exact number of *Dolois* and *Syiems* before the advent of the British, available records reveal that the British had recognized 20 *dolois* in Jaintia Hills and 25 out of the 30 States and 31 *'Sirdarships'* in the Khasi Hills. Out of the 25 Khasi States, 16 were known as *Syiemships*, 3 as *Lyngdohships*, 5 as *Sirdarships* and 1 as *Wahadadarship*. The 31 *Sirdarships* were called 'British villages' (Mathew, 1980). Tax on Land has always been unknown among the vast majority of Khasis.[14] In spite of British possession, some of the Khasi States sought protection from the British. There was no instance of the British substantially interfering with the tribal rights to land. Strictly speaking, the British generally did not interfere with the customary laws and practices of the people the governed.[15]

British administration showed considerable respect for customary land laws of the Khasis and never stood in the way of its normal operation. The Meghalaya Land and Reforms Manual while expressing its viewpoint on this matter noted, "The customs of the Khasis in regard to land was respected by the British from the day they came to these hills in 1829 till the day they departed in 1947. We may be surprised by the magnanimity of the British, strange though it may sound that they never thought it necessary to interfere in the customs of the Khasis. For their needs and requirements of land the British went through proper negotiations, after due agreements, paid for the land in cash" (Phira, 1989).

However, there were some instances which showed hostility demands by the colonial authority especially with regard to dealings concerned with transaction of land. This was evident in the series of rebellions staged by the Jaintias of Jaintia Hills which led to the imposition of taxation system by the British in order to put the chiefs under control. Following this imposition the Jaintias humbly complied with the order by paying the taxes, but in course of time their frustration made way for the historic Jaintia Rebellion of 1862.

A careful study of the Khasi Land Tenure system reveals some startling facts about the ambiguity of ownership and control of land. Thus with the attainment of statehood, one of the first functions of the government of Meghalaya was to make a detailed study of the land holding operations prevalent among the Khasis with a view towards codification of the customary land laws. The land tenure system in its intermediate state as at present is the most vexed questions amongst the Khasis, affecting their entire life because of their historical attachment to the land (Report of the Land Reforms Commission for Khasi Hills, 1975). From time immemorial land has always belonged, and is still held to belong, to the people and neither to the rulers nor the Government. Accordingly, the government of Meghalaya appointed the Land Reforms Commission in 1973 to bring about a logical order of the Khasi land tenure system and its related concepts of ownership, control and occupancy rights of land.

Categories of Land and the Land Tenure System

The Commission has dealt with three categories of land in the Khasi Hills, viz., Community Land known as *Ri Raid*, Privately owned land called *Ri Kynti* and Government land.

1. *Ri Raid (Community Land)*

Ri Raid is Community Land which is managed and controlled

by the concerned community. Every member of the community has the right of use and occupancy of the *Ri Raid* land without payment of land revenue. The community may be a village, a group of villages or an *elaka*. No person has proprietary, heritable or transferable rights over such land. He has only the right of use and occupancy, and such rights revert to the community when the person ceases to occupy or use the land for a period of three years or more. The only way in which a person can inherit land or obtain transferable rights over such land is by making permanent improvements on the land in the form of permanent buildings or cultivation of permanent crops and plant like fruit trees or cultivation. But these rights lapse if he abandons the land over a long period.

Ri Raid land comprises many sub-classes which can be categorized as forest lands and non-forest lands.

Forest lands are of the following kinds:

1. *Ri 'Law Kyntang, Ri 'Law Niam or Ri 'Law Lyngdoh* : These are forests in *Raid* lands set apart for religious purposes, managed and controlled by the Raid or the village or in the case of the *Ri Law Lyngdoh* by the *Lyngdoh* (Priest) of the community.
2. *Ri 'Law Adong, Ri 'Law Sang, Ri 'Law Shnong* : These are village forests reserved by the villagers so that any member could obtain timber or firewood for personal needs or for use as water catchment areas.
3. *Ri 'Law Sumar* : Which belongs to the individual, clan or the village who had first occupied and afforested then and maintains them thereafter.

Non-forest lands include the following types of land:

1. *Ri Shnong* (Village land) : It is a *raid* land forming part of the village and can be utilised by any member of the village.

2. *Ri Umsnam* (land acquired through war) : It is a *raid* land which an '*elaka*' had won in the older days 'by the sword'.
3. *Ri Ialeh Mukotdama* (land acquired through litigation) : Those lands which have been acquired through litigation by an *elaka*.
4. *Ri Bamlang* (land given by the *Syiem*) : Any land when given over to the community by the *Syiem*.
5. *Ri Bam Syiem* (land used by the *Syiem*) : Any *raid* land which has been set apart for the exclusive use of the ruling chief and his clan (*kurs*).
6. *Ri Aitimon Sngewbha* : Any land gifted by private landowners to the community for public use.

2. *Ri Kynti (Private Land)*

'*Kynti*' means 'absolute possession'. Therefore, *Ri Kynti* lands are private lands which have been acquired by a man or woman individually, or in the case of a woman, inherited from her mother. Such lands must entirely be distinguished from lands of the clan. Colonel Gurdon notes that privately held lands "may be sub-divided into *Ri-Kur* or lands which are property of the clan, *Ri-Kynti*, family or acquired land property". The clan lands, originally when the population was sparse, were owned by families but as the members of the family increased and a clan was formed out of the increasing number of families sprung from a common ancestress, the lands became the property of the clan instead of the family. Such clan lands are properly demarcated by boundary marks.

Like the *Ri Raid* Land, *Ri Kynti* Land comprises many sub-classes:

1. *Ri Kur* (Land belonging to a Clan) : It is a *Ri Kynti* land which has not yet been divided among the different branches of a clan or among different families of a branch

of a clan. This land is apportionable by a ***dorbar kur*** (clan council) or ***dorbar kpoh*** (council of a branch of the clan) as the case may be.

2. *Ri Nongtymmen* (Land owned by Inheritance) : Is *Ri Kynti* Land which has descended from generation to generation usually after two or three generations. This land is divisible or apportionable by a ***dorbar*** of the clan or by a branch of the clan if already divided among the several branches thereof. The head of the family, i.e. the mother may also divide this land among her children, usually daughters.

3. *Ri Maw* (Stone Land or Land acquired by Purchase) : Is *Ri Kynti* Land acquired by right of purchase or by right of apportionment among the member of the family or of the clan and the holders thereof have the right to erect boundary stones to demarcate their respective lots.

4. *Ri Seng :* Is *Ri Kynti* Land acquired from ancient time by a number of different clans or families and has not been divided. Income from this land is divided among the households of the clans or families holding it. The management of *Ri Seng* is in the hands of the representative elected by members of all owing clans or families. In certain cases, such lands may also devolve on male descendants when the clan or families have become extinct, that is when their female relations have died leaving no female issues.

5. *Ri Dakhol* (Land obtained by purchase or right of occupation) : Is land over which a person has obtained *Ri Kynti* rights by right of occupation and mauling permanent improvements thereon or by right of purchase or winning a court case.

6. *Ri Shyieng* (Land used for religious rites by the *khadduh*) : Is a portion of *Ri kur* specially allotted to *Ka Khadduh* (youngest daughter) of a clan or a family to

enable her to meet the expenses connected with the performance of religious rites ceremonies concerning the clan, *kpoh* or family, like depositing of the ashes of the dead in the co-urns of the clan. Such land is generally given to *Ka Khadduh* as an additional share.

7. *Ri Lyngdoh* : Is *Ri Kynti* land of the *Lyngdoh* or Priest of a particular native state.
8. *Ri Syiem* : Is *Ri Kynti* land of the *Syiem's* clan. In some *syiemships* it can be Raid Land set apart for maintenance of the *Syiem's* clan.
9. *Ri Iapduh* (Land of a clan that has become extinct) : Is *Ri Kynti* land of a clan or a family which has become extinct. Such land according to the time-honoured custom reverts to the chief who is immune from a curse on that family but who will keep it for the *elaka* as *Ri Raid* or as *Ri Bam Syiem* for the family of a ruling chief (Report of the Land Reforms Commission).

CLASSIFICATIONS OF FOREST LANDS IN MEGHALAYA

In Meghalaya, forest may be classified in a number of ways such as by composition, legal status, ownership, exploitation and functions.[16] However, as far as uses of the word forest is concerned, in Meghalaya it is found to be interpreted in the following three ways:

1. Forest Area
2. Forest Cover
3. Forest by Use

1. *Forest Area*

Here refers to the area recorded as "forest" in the government records, often this term is also written as "recorded forest area".[17]

The recorded forest area in Meghalaya is categorised into "Reserved Forest", "Protected Forest" and "Unclassed Forest".

(i) *Reserved Forest (RF) :* These forests are managed and directly controlled by the State Government. These areas are notified under the provisions of Indian Forest Act or the State Forest Acts having full degree of protection. In Reserved Forests all activities are prohibited unless permitted.

(ii) *Protected Forest (PF) :* These forests are notified under the provisions of Indian Forest Act or the State Forest Acts having limited degree of protection. In protected forest all activities are permitted unless prohibited.

(iii) *Unclassed Forest (UF) or District Council Reserve Forest :* These forests are not included in reserved or protected forests category and ownership status of such forests varies from state to state. In Meghalaya they are directly controlled and managed by the District Councils under the Sixth Schedule to the Indian Constitution. All private forests or village forests are included in the unclassed forest.

The recorded forest area of Meghalaya is 9,496 sq. km or 42.34 pe rcent of the state's geographical area comprising 1,112 sq. km of Reserved Forest, 12 sq. km of protected forest and 8,372 sq. km of Unclassed Forest Table 1.1

This distribution is depicted in Fig. 1.1 representing distribution of forest area in the state.

Table 1.1 : Distribution of forest area in Meghalaya

Recorded Forest Area	
Reserved Forest (RF)	1,112 km^2
Protected Forest (PF)	12 km^2
Unclassed Forest (UF)	8,372 km^2
Total	9,496 km^2
Of State Geographic Area	*42.3%*
Of Country's Forest Area	*1.2%*

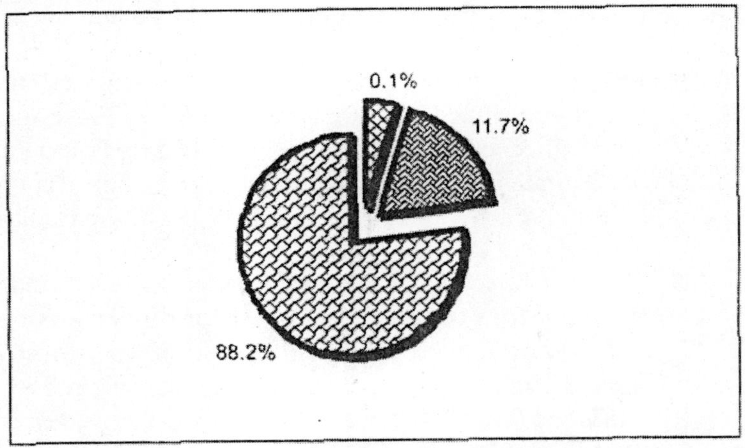

Fig. 1.1: PIE CHART : Distribution of forest area in Meghalaya.

Table 1.2 : District-wise Forest Cover (Meghalaya) (Area in Km²)

District	*Geographical area*	*Forest Cover*				*Scrub*
		Dense forest	*Open forest*	*Total*	*Per cent*	
East Garo Hills[TH]	2,603					
South Garo Hills[TH]	1,849	1,038	2,737	3,775	84.79	8
East Khasi Hills[TH]	2,820	997	1,553	2,550	90.43	29
Jaintia Hills[TH]	3,819	890	1,047	1,937	50.72	117
Ri Bhoi[TH]	2,376	656	1,107	1,763	74.20	68
West Garo Hills[TH]	3,715	1,002	1,590	2,592	69.77	3
West Khasi Hills[TH]	5,247	1,098	1,869	2,967	56.55	34
Total	**22,429**	**5,681**	**9,903**	**15,584**	**69.48**	**259**

Source: State of Forest Report 2001.

2. *Forest Cover*

Consists of all lands more than 1 ha area having tree canopy density of more than 10 per cent irrespective of the tree species and its legal status or ownership or land use that can be interpreted from satellite data published by the National Remote Sensing Agency (NRSA) while interpreting satellite data, one can distinguish between reflectance of tree vegetation from other land cover, but it is not possible to know from the image what kind of land use is being practiced under the tree cover or who owns the land. Thus land use or ownership cannot be taken into consideration while classifying forest cover for example, delineating tree lands as orchards, coffee/tea plantations, public parks, agro forestry plantations etc.

Further Forest cover is classified into two classes, namely:

(1) *Dense forest :* Which includes all lands with a forests cover of trees with a canopy density of over 40 per cent?

(2) *Open forest :* Which includes all lands with a forest cover of trees with a canopy density between 10 to 40 per cent. Besides the category 'forest cover' there is the 'non-forest' category which includes all lands without forest cover, such as agricultural croplands, grasslands, wastelands, scrub, water bodies, riverbeds, snow-covered mountains and built up areas. Only 'scrub' has been classified as a separate class within "non-forest". Scrub denotes lands having bushes and/or poor tree growth with canopy density less than 10 per cent. Such lands are delineated largely within or around continuous forest areas.

The State/UT-wise forest cover in the country is shown in Table 1.3, where Meghalaya has 5,681 sq. km. of Dense Forest cover and 9,903 sq. km. presented a paper on "Dynamics of Coal and Limestone Extraction in Meghalaya. A "Comparative Analysis" of open forest cover as against the total geographical area of 22,327 sq. km.

Change in Forest Cover

Monitoring the forest cover of the country on a two-year cycle, the FSI reports that the term "Change" denotes the net change in the status of forest cover determining either an increase or decrease in the forest cover during the period intervening the

Table 1.3 : State/UT-wise Forest Cover in Hill Districts

State / UT	*No. of Hill Districts*	*Geographical area in Hill Districts*	*Forest Cover*			*Forest Cover (%)*
			Dense	*Open*	*Total*	
Arunachal Pradesh	13	83,743	53932	14113	68045	81.25
Assam	3	19,153	7175	5849	13024	68.00
Himachal Pradesh	12	55,673	10429	3931	14360	25.79
J & K	14	222,236	11850	9389	21237	9.56
Karnataka	6	48,046	19100	4953	24053	50.06
Kerela	10	29,572	9830	3141	12971	43.86
Maharashtra	7	69,905	7886	4126	12012	17.18
Manipur	*9*	*22,327*	*5710*	*11216*	*16926*	*75.81*
Meghalaya	7	22,429	5,681	9,903	15,584	69.48
Mizoram	8	21,081	8936	8558	17494	82.98
Nagaland	8	16,579	5,393	7,952	13,345	80.49
Sikkim	4	7,096	2,391	802	3,193	45.00
Tamil Nadu	5	22,789	3555	2328	5883	25.82
Tripura	3	10,486	3,502	3,563	7,065	67.38
Uttarakhand	13	53,483	19,023	4,915	23,938	44.76
West Bengal	1	3,149	1,417	779	2,196	69.74
Total	123	707,747	175,771	95,557	217,236	38.34

Table 1.4 : Forest Cover in Meghalaya

Forest Cover	
Dense Forest	5,681 km²
Open Forest	9,903 km²
Total	15,584 km²
Of State Geographic Area	*69.5%*
Of Country's Forest Cover	2.3%

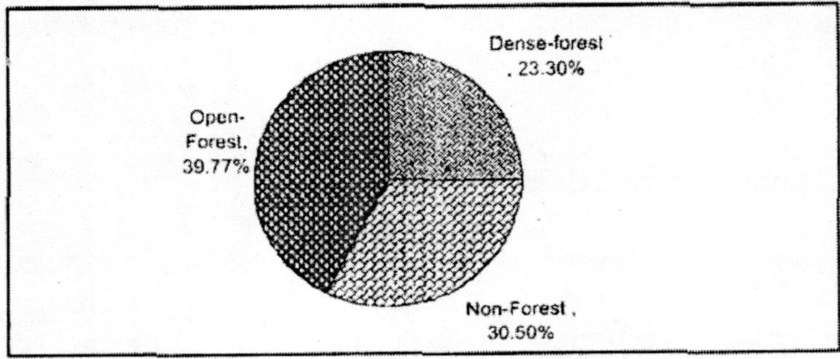

Fig. 1.2 : PIE CHART: Forest Cover in Meghalaya

two assessments. Table 1.5 shows net change in the extent of forest cover in Meghalaya between 1999 to 2001.

Table 1.5: Change in Forest Cover

1999 Assessment			*2001 Assessment*			*Net difference*
Dense	*Open*	*Total*	*Dense*	*Open*	*Total*	
5,925	9,708	15,633	5,681	9,903	15,584	-49 sq. km.

3. *Forest by Use*

Excludes those areas used for non-forestry purposes, typically *jhumming* and non-forest area etc.

We have seen above the three basic uses of the term forest in Meghalaya, viz. forest cover, forest area and forest by use. Besides this there are other legal classifications of forest in Meghalaya provided by various Commissions and Acts passed by the Government such as the following.

I. Land Reforms Commission Report (1974) on the Categorisation of Land in Khasi Hills

1. *Ri Law kyntang, Ri law Lyngdoh and Ri Law Niam*

These are forests in Raid lands that are set apart for religious purposes, managed and controlled in the case of *Ri Law Lyngdoh* by the *Lyngdoh* and in the case of *Ri Law Kyntang* or *Law Niam* by the Raid of the village.

2. *Ri Law Sumar*

It is a forest within the Raid lands belonging to an individual, a family, a clan or a village community as a whole depending on who first afforests the land and maintains the forest.

3. *Ri Law Adong, Ri Law Sang and Ri Law Shnong*

These are village forests reserved by the villagers as water catchment areas or to enable members of the village or Raid as the case may be to get firewood or timber for their personal needs or for any such purposes as the village or Raid durbar may decide from time to time.

II. Khasi Hills Autonomous District (Management and Control of Forests) Act, 1958

According to the Act the following types of forest have been identified:

1. *Private Forests*

These forests are owned and managed by an individual or clan or a joint clan. They are either grown or inherited in recognised private lands (*Ri Kynti*).

2. *Green Block*

These are forests belonging to an individual family or clan or joint clan and Raid lands already declared as Green Block by the Government for aesthetic beauty and water supply of the town of Shillong and its suburbs.

3. *Raid Forests*

These are forests looked after by the heads of the Raid under the management of the local administrative heads.

4. *District Council Reserved Forests*

These are forests that may be so declared by the Executive Committee and shall be owned, managed, controlled by the Executive Committee.

5. *Unclassed Forests*

These are forests hitherto known as Unclassed State Forests

before the commencement of the Constitution of India directly managed and controlled by the Government including any other forest(s) not falling within any of the above classification.[18]

The Classification of forestlands by the Land Reforms Commission Report and the Khasi Hills Autonomous District Council showed that ownership, control and management is the community, clan or private. The exact size of such of these classified forestlands is not known.

The District Councils besides controlling and managing some forestlands are also given constitutional power to make laws over the tribal areas. The Act of 1980 passed by the District Council states that the Community, clan and private forests must be registered with details of ownership and boundaries; the trees and any forest products from these forests cannot be disposed by way of sale, mortgage, base, gift or otherwise without the approval of the competent authority of the District Council. The application of disposal of trees or any produce must be routed through the traditional heads who shall forward to the Chief Forest Officer (CFO) of the District Council. The Act does not in any manner deal with the internal mechanism of rights of use of the common property. It is left to the traditional institutions.

GENERAL ACCOUNT OF FOREST TYPES OF MEGHALAYA

There is a rich literary account on the diverse vegetational cover of North East India through the works of eminent botanists and forest officers such as Hooker (1854, 1872-97, 1904); Griffith (1848); Clarke (1889); Kanjilal *et al.* (1934-40); Champion (1936); Bor (1938, 1942); Biswas (1941, 1943); Das (1942); Rowntree (1954); Puri (1960); Kingdon Ward (1960); Rajkhowa (1961); Rao (1961); Champion and Seth (1968); Legris (1963); Rao (1968, 1974); Balakrishnan (1981-83) and Rao (1982). However studies, with particular reference to forest types of Meghalaya are scanty (Rao, 1968, 1974; Bor,

1942; Joseph, 1968; Balakrishnan, 1981; Baishya and Rao, 1982; Sarma, 2003 etc.).

Based on these fragmentary studies, as well as from the present study, the forests of Meghalaya can be broadly grouped under the following types:

I. Tropical Forests

These forests are met within areas up to an elevation of 1200 m. and with an average rainfall of about 100–250 cm. There are numerous sub-types within this category, such as evergreen, semi-evergreen, moist and dry deciduous forests etc.

(a) Tropical Evergreen Forests

This category of forest is confined to upper reaches of hill range beginning from Tura range extended up to Siju forest reserved. These forests usually occur in high rainfall areas as well as near catchment areas. They harbour a very rich species diversity where nature is at its extravaganza forming a closed evergreen canopy. Though these forests are not completely free from human interference due to *jhum* practice and seldom form continuous belts, yet the species available here are mighty and often blanketed by lush growth of tropical flora.

(b) Tropical Semi-evergreen Forests

This category of forests occupy the north-eastern and northern slopes of the state, typically up to elevations of 1200 m., where annual rainfall is 150–200 cm. with a comparatively cooler winter. The number of species here are fewer than the evergreen zone. The areas of Saipung and Narpuh reserved forests fall under this category. The dominant trees in these forests are mostly deciduous species[19] such as *Careya arborea*, *Dillenia pentagyna* and *Callicarpa arborea*.

(c) Tropical Moist and Dry Deciduous Forests

This type of forests occurs where annual rainfall is below 150 cm and at comparatively low elevations. Typical natural deciduous forests do not occur anywhere in Meghalaya but are only sub-climax or man-made forests.

These forests are characterised by seasonal leaf shedding and profuse flowering of the trees. Recurrent forest fires are a common phenomenon here. Deciduous forests are much more extensive in their distribution in the state and include a host of economically important trees like *Shorea robusta*, *Tectona grandis*, *Artocarpus chaplasha* etc. These types of forests are prevalent at lower elevations in Garo Hills, lower Khasi and Jaintia Hills under hot and humid climatic condition. Apart from mixed deciduous forests there are bamboo intruded deciduous forests where a good number of bamboos grow. Bamboo forests are not natural but appear in *jhum* fallows of 15–20 years. These forests at places form pure stands. The common bamboo species in Meghalaya are *Dendrocalamus hamiltonii*, *D. gigantea*, *Bambusa bambos*, *Cephalostachyum latifolium*, *Chimonobambusa khasiana*, *Melocanna bambusoides* etc. Bamboos also appear in comparatively older forests where there are some gaps in the canopy.

II. Grasslands and Savannas

Grasslands of Meghalaya are also not of a climax type but are only as a result of removal of original forest cover. The rolling grasslands covering large areas can be seen throughout the Shillong plateau, around Riangdo, Ranikor, Weiloi, Mawphlang, Mawsynram, Cherrapunji, Shillong-Jowai, Jarain and Sutnga in Khasi and Jaintia Hills and major parts of West Garo Hills. Apart from giving a green look to these barren hills, these grasslands also support other dicotyledonous species.

III. Sub-tropical Pine Forests

The pine forests in Meghalaya are confined to higher reaches of the Shillong plateau in Khasi and Jaintia Hills, in a narrow belt showing an east-west direction. *Pinus kesiya* is the principal species, often forming pure strands. Pine forests of Meghalaya are, however, not a climax type, but are of secondary nature and is in a stage of succession termination.[20]

IV. Sal Forest

These forests occupy the northern part of Khasi Hills with pure varieties growing in certain parts of Garo Hills. The Rongrengiri Reserve forest is considered to be the best Sal reserve in India (Sarma, 2003:169). Bamboo forests grow within Sal forests. The wood from Sal (*Shorea robusta*) is generally used for the construction of furniture, railway tract and sleepers etc.

Classification of forest types in any terrain is such as directly related to environmental factors such as climate, physiography and edaphic (soil). These three factors play a vital role in the growth of particular species of trees and plant vegetation. For example, the climatic elements of temperature, rainfall, relative humidity etc. could be favourable to a particular plant growth over a considerable period. In the Central and Eastern upland of Meghalaya, sub-tropical moist hill (pine) type of forests is predominant and the dominant tree is pine (*Pinus kesiya*) (Sarma, 2003: 109).

REFERENCES

1. Bareh, Hamlet. 1985. *The History and Culture of the Khasi People*. Guwahati : Spectrum Publications, p. 10.
2. *Ibid.*, p. 9
3. Gurdon, P.R.T. 1975. *The Khasis*. Delhi: Cosmo Publications. p.11.
4. Bareh, Hamlet. 1985. *The History and Culture of the Khasi People*. Guwahati : Spectrum Publications,p.13.
5. *Ibid.*, p.15.
6. Sarma, Sidheswar. 2003. *Meghalaya the Land and Forest : A Remote Sensing Based Study*. Guwahati: Geophil Publishing House, p. 73.

7. *Shillong Times*,Vol. IV, No. 142. Shillong, November 7, 2000.
8. *Apphira Daily News*, Vol. III, No. 83. Shillong, May 14, 1997.
9. *Apphira Daily News*, Vol.III, No.83.Shillong, May 14, 1997.
10. Nongbri, Tiplut. 2003. *Development, Ethnicity and Gender: Select Essays on Tribes in India*. New Delhi: Rawat Publications.
11. *Ibid.*, p.123.
12. Mathew, T. 1980. *Tribal Economy of North-Eastern Region*. Guwahati: Spectrum Publications, p. 36.
13. *Ibid.*, p. 56.
14. *The Assam Land Revenue Manual*, Vol. I, 7th Edition, 1965.
15. Nongbri, Tiplut. 2003. *Development, Ethnicity and Gender : Select Essays on Tribes in India*. New Delhi: Rawat Publications, p. 124.
16. Sinha, A.C. 1993. *Beyond the Trees, Tigers and Tribes: Historical Sociology of the Eastern Himalayan Forests*. New Delhi : Har Anand Publications, p. 21.
17. State of Forest Report 2001, Forest Survey of India, 2001, pp. 5-6.
18. Khasi Hills Autonomous District Council.1995.*The United Khasi–Jaintia Hills Autonomous District (Management and Control of Forests)Act 1958.*Shillong : Ibani Printing Press, p. 6.
19. *Ibid.*, p. 166.
20. Sarma, Sidheswar. 2003 *Meghalaya the Land and Forest: A Remote Sensing Based Study*. Guwahati: Geophil Publishing House, p. 109.

2 PEOPLE AND FORESTS IN KHASI HILLS

The forest or '*ki khlaw ki btap*' as the Khasis name it, has since time immemorial endured as a revered entity. Looking closely at the value system of the Khasi, one finds that it is centred on the Supreme Being, (*U Blei Nongbuh, Nongthaw*) as well as the transmigration of the soul and religious doctrines, which govern the family and social life. Their relation with God is one of esteemed reverence and fear and they believe that God confidently entrusts and commits to them the basic requirements necessary for their survival and provides all their needs. Thus forest, as a natural resource with its bountiful products is freely accessible to humanity.

For a Khasi, the forest is a well loved home, a game sanctuary and also an abode of worship all rolled into one, around which his social, cultural and religious activities revolve. The Khasis bestow a deep sense of veneration and respect on nature, which has been rightly acclaimed by a famous Khasi writer H.O. Mawrie in the following words:

"U Khasi u im bad ka mariang, bad ka mariang ka im bad u".

This resounding declaration when translated means, "A Khasi lives with nature and nature lives with him".

This statement bears testimony to the fact that nature with all its bounty shares a harmonious relationship with the Khasis.

While delving deeper into the environmental history of the Khasis, one is struck by the close affinity that exists between the three entities of "God", "Nature" and "Man". This is conclusive evidence to the fact that the Khasis uphold an eco-theandric vision of reality where God, Nature and Man form one single and indivisible entity. The earth is honoured and idolized as "*Meiramew*" which literally means 'mother earth'; *Meiramew*, being combination of land, forest, rivers and streams, the Khasis do not divide these elements as separate entities. While God is present in nature, on the hills, mountains, rivers, lakes, forests, etc. man forms an integral part of this natural environment. Thus there is an inseparable relationship between God, Man and the objects of Nature. The Khasis sanctify nature and all its elements as gifts from God.

The eco-theandric vision of nature as a universal feature of the religion of the tribals has been well formulated and used by L.P Vidyarthi to describe the ethnography of the sacred city of Gaya and the religious life of the Maler, a tribal community.[1] The three concepts : (i) a 'Sacred geography', (ii) a set of 'sacred perfomances' and (iii) a corps of 'sacred specialists' are collectively conceived, and termed by the Malers as a "Sacred Complex". Thus, one finds a similar expression of the 'wholeness of nature' as an abode of spirits in both the Khasis and the Malers.

FOREST : A SACRED ENTITY

The supernatural connotations of forest have occupied an important place in Khasi literature, Khasi legends and folktales and the life and culture of the people as a whole. This 'sacred' character of the forest finds expression in the customary practice of preserving sacred groves known as 'Law kyntang', which are held with high esteem even today.

SACRED GROVES OR LAW KYNTANG : AN ECOLOGICAL LEGACY

The forest culture of the Khasis is deeply rooted in the age-old practice of sacred groves that can still be found in areas of Khasi-Jaintia Hills.These fully developed virgin forest patches are known by different names in Meghalaya. In Khasi they are known as ***Law Kyntang***, ***Law Lyngdoh*** and ***Law Niam***, in Jaintia they are called ***Khloo Blai***, ***Khloo Blai Lyngdoh*** and ***Kanggimin Bol Waarangni Biap*** and *Asang Khosi* among the Garos. Research has found that a total of 79 groves have been documented in Meghalaya covering an estimated 10,251 ha. Out of which 32 are found in East Khasi Hills, 13 in West Khasi Hills and 15 in Jaintia Hills, eight each in the East and West Garo Hills and three in Ri-Bhoi district. At first glance, these groves appear to be impenetrable, dark green masses that have remained unchanged for years. But a walk into the woods reveals a grand epic that unfolds the region's oral history that is attuned to forest.

It has not been an easy task to date the origin of the sacred groves, as most scientists say that the pre-agrarian age might have been the starting point. D.D. Kosambi, in 1962 referred to a similar pattern of bio-diversity management found elsewhere in the country. B.K. Roy Burman, the Delhi based anthropologist talked of the sacred groves in Meghalaya as being created not for bio-diversity but for the king-priests, to extend protection to the traders,who travelled on international routes.It is still not known as to whether the Khasis consciously commited theses forests to be refugia but this functional role of sacred groves happened at a time when dense forests and thick jungles were freely available and bio-diversity conservation was only incidental. Therefore, though the myth of the origin sacred groves is shrouded in mystery, one cannot undermine its importance as a treasure house and repository of rich flora and fauna.

The nature of beliefs and rituals associated with sacred groves have made the Khasis to view their forests as 'sacrosanct'. Not a tree shall be cut, nor a stone or leaf removed from these forests.Whoever causes sacrilege, will fall under the curse of the forest deity or *U Ryngkew U Basa*.This reverential attitude on entering the forest is strictly followed by the Khais even today. It is intersting to note that the Khasis assign a great deal of cultural and symbolic importance to the sacred groves. This is manifested in the many rituals and ceremonies performed within the premises of these groves to appease the Gods.

(a) Sacred Groves as Location for Cultural and Religious Activities

These groves have been the site of rituals, taboos and ceremonies, a locale where social moral values are passed on to the younger generation. These groves house the most important religious and ritual relics. The Khasis believe that the guardian spirit of U Ryngkew U Basa is present in these groves since time immemorial and as the name suggests the spirit takes care and protects the people from sickness, pain and invasion by enemies. Destroying or cuttting of trees from the grove is prohibited as this would go against the wishes of U Ryngkew U Basa. There are some common rituals held every year in the groves which bring to light the deep sense of reverence that the Khasis have towards forests:

Ka Leh Niam Pyrda is a religious ritual held every year in the month of April by the *Lyngdoh Syntiew* clan. This ritual is performed in a particular location inside the deep groves. In this ceremony, it is customary to choose an odd number of members (7-9) comprising all males selected from different clans of the village. The ceremony is started by the Lyngdoh who sacrifices a white cock after which other items such as rice beer, fish, prawns and ginger are also used as offerings to the spirit. After successful completion of the ritual, the lyngdoh feasts with the other male counterparts.

In the sacred groves at Raliang, Jaintia Hills, a religious ceremony performed annually is known as *Ka Nguh Blai* or bowing in front of God, which is held every year during April and November. The Jaintia priest (*Bamon*) goes on a fast for the first 2 days before the festival after which there is a dance called '*Pastieh*' exclusively performed by the menfolk. Offerings like pumpkin, sugarcane and a black goat are offered to the Goddess *Kepati* after which the day concludes. On the second day of the ceremony, the *Bamon* accompanied by the *Nongkynrih* drums walks down the river '*Umioorem*' to seek blessings from the Goddess by offering a bunch of flowers and a pigeon to the river.

(b) Sacred Groves as Housing Spirits

While the Khasis do not deify nature as God, they believe in the existence of "spirits" that are believed to hover or roam around and inhabit the natural surroundings. These spirits are held with great awe and reverence and a Khasi would spare no pains to appease these spirits, because they are looked upon as powerful influences in nature.

The Khasis divide the realm of spirits into two categories according to their intention towards mankind. The spirits with good intention are regarded as godlings or "*Lei*". Each of these godlings presides over a specific function. These deities are supposed to be associated with functions as state welfare, wealth, water, village, etc. The spirits with bad intention are referred to as '*suid*' and are responsible for causing harm and injury, sickness or even death. The Khasis believe that the good spirits protect them only as long as they obey God's commands, but the moment they cease to obey, the evil forces will interfere with their lives in many ways and harm them. Thus they would speak of a number of spirits associated with objects of nature such as:

- Mountain or hill spirits (*Lei Lum*)
- River spirits (*Lei Wah*)
- Forest spirits (*Lei Khlaw*)
- God of the state (*Lei Mulluk*)
- Water spirits (*Lei Umtong*).

The forest is considered as an abode of the '*lei*' or good spirits where the '*rngai*' or shadow of the deceased roams about. Therefore, while wandering through the woods, mountains and valleys, it is customary for a Khasi to do so with respect and develop a feeling of reverence towards the natural surroundings.

(c) Symbolic and Sacred Significance of Particular Forest Resources

It has been found that specific forest resources such as species of trees and plants, bamboo and leaves link the Khasis to a particular religious belief and symbol. A particular type of tree called *'khnong'* is held sacred by the Khasi-Pnars. The tree is worshipped for a fruitful harvest and a plentiful year. The Khasi oak or *'dieng-sning'* also acquires an important place in Khasi rites and rituals. During the occurrence of an epidemic or *jingiap khlam*, the *lyngdoh* (Khasi priest) conducts a sacrifice where a goat, a hen, powdered rice and a gourd of fermented liquor, along with the leaves of the *dieng sning* are used at this ceremony.

Uses of Certain Species of Trees

1. Ka Kain (Succedaneae)

This is a big tree with large fruits, which the birds are very fond of. It produces to the one who touches it, itching and ulcers. Timber from this tree is used for making a musical instrument called *'Duitara'* because it is light in weight and gives out sweet tune by its soft and vibrating quality. When the makers of the *duitara* go out in the woods to cut the tree, they utter a few words to please the tree spirits.

They say, "*Hey nga ibha ia pha*", which means "Oh! I love you", this is done before they even touch the tree because they believe that if they say so the tree will not produce itching in their bodies.

2. Ka Dieng Jri (Urticeceae; Ficus hispida)

This is a very useful tree for the Khasis. They take this tree in a high esteem and many villages prohibit cutting down this tree. In village Nongjri there were many trees of this species which were used for collecting latex and export it outside for industrial use.

This tree, which gives out many roots from its branches and are very strong and long, the Khasis use to plant the trees on either side of a river and when they become matured with a number of roots hanging from their branches, they draw them from bank to bank and construct suspension bridges with branches and canes.

3. Ka Sangniah (Euphorbiaceae bridalia)

This tree is available in the plain areas and is very unique and useful as its timber is soft and can be given any delicate shape. It does not crack in the sun and wind. Khasi artisans use to make many useful household articles like spoons, forks, dishes, combs, musical instruments and decorative works of art.

4. Ka Dieng Jakrai

This tree was used in the olden days by the Khasi artisans to make rice plates and other household articles with this timber. The fibers of this timber are said to be very smooth and do not break easily while cutting in delicate designs. Secondly, it has a natural brown colour and therefore requires no painting. Thirdly, it does not crack or break in the heat of the sun.

Superstitions, Taboos Pertaining to Trees and Timber

The Khasis believe in the existence of a forest spirit, *U 'suid br'* or *U 'suid khlaw*. The Khasi word '*Sang*' implies an interdiction either religious or social from doing any particular thing.[2] There are special taboos set aside with regard to the use of wood or timber. The following are some, which are held lightly today:

1. To build a house with resinous timber. Only the syiem family can use such timber.
2. To cut trees from a sacred Forest.
3. To use more than one kind of timber in building the hearth.
4. Trees or branches of trees falling on our way may bring bad luck to either maternal or paternal kins.[3]

FOREST WISDOM OF THE KHASIS

The ecological wisdom of the Khasis is a wisdom that is solidly based on "experience" and they depend on this knowledge to fulfil most of their day to day needs (their economy). Through agriculture, hunting, fishing and gathering a huge range of forest foods and materials is acquired with which they make most of their articles of daily use, from houses to ploughs, baskets to leaf-plates. They possess an ancient lore of herbal medicine (***dawai kynbat***) which is found to be very effective remedies for various sicknesses. Their ability to predict diseases from elements of nature and to differentiate between edible and wild plants is notable. Much of this ancient wisdom is today the result of oral tradition. Forest wisdom has enabled the Khasis to live in harmony with nature besides elevating them to such a high pedestal that no animal or living creature could compete with. The following examples throw light on the use of such forest knowledge in understanding what happens in the natural surroundings:

1. The Khasis believe that the flowering of bamboo is a sign that famine is close at hand because it would attract rats that would then be detrimental to farming and cultivation.
2. The pine tree for a Khasi is a symbol of goodwill, nobleness and self-sacrifice because it provides fuel, timber, leaves, etc.
3. When tender leaves start growing on rubber trees, it is indicative that fishes are multiplying in rivers and seas.
4. When the petals of a particular flower called '*kymbat samthiah*' close, the sun begins to set and when the petals open, the sun rises.
5. The flowering of a particular plant called '*tiew diengsong*' in the month of September is associated with the onset of fever.

Thus there are lessons to be learnt from the signs of nature. Much of the forest knowledge of the Khasis has been lost today due to the advancement of science and the diminishing role of oral tradition. However, the Khasis still uphold their natural wisdom, which helps them in unveiling the mysteries of life.

KHASI RURAL WOMEN AND FOREST LIVELIHOOD

The importance of women in collection of forest produce is borne by data from almost every country in Asia, Africa and Latin America. For instance a study in the North-west Frontier Province of Pakistan showed that 78 per cent of morel mushrooms are collected by women and children. Similarly, in West Bengal, tribal women gather Sal (Shorea Robusta) leaves for six months of the year and make about Rs.72 per month under the best circumstances. Throughout India, collection of tendu leaves(*Diospyros Melanoxylon*)generates part-time employment for 7.5 million people –a majority of them tribal women.

All these studies indicate that women spend more time and labour in forest related activities and depend on forests not only to meet subsistence needs but also for income. Interestingly, the considerable role played by women in ensuring food security and in the provision of cash income from the sale of NTFPs (Non-Timber Forest Products) gives women a higher status in tribal societies. The vast range of literature on gender and forest has repeatedly shown that women's connections with forest resources are related to their subsistence use and therefore, deforestation and forest degradation has a more direct effect on the lives of women than on their counterparts.

As nurtures of family line, Khasi women have had a significant role to play in the domestic sphere.[4] Her familial roles are well defined and her "glorifying status" as a mother has furthered her roles and responsibilities towards meeting the immediate needs of the family. These roles include some burdensome duties and responsibilities which are part of their household chores such as carrying water, fetching firewood, washing clothes, collecting twigs and edible plants and roots which are carried out in the jungle skirting the village. This has partly been borne out of the fact that women have had a closer interaction with nature and this has enhanced the emotional bond with nature since it has helped them cope up with a number of economic hardships.

The following are the main parameters of forest dependency by the Khasi rural women:

(a) Fuel and Fodder Needs

Firewood is the main energy source in the rural areas. It is another forest product on which the households are dependent. The twigs, branches of most of the forest species and the bushes and other wastes are collected from the forest and used for fuel purpose by the household in and near the forests. Firewood and charcoal are indispensable sources of energy used in every Khasi household for cooking, heating and drying purposes. Data collected from Lawbyrwa village in Ri-Bhoi district shows that 20.56 per cent of adult workers are engaged in cutting and selling firewood and 22.22 per cent of them eke out their livelihood by making and selling charcoal.

(b) Other NTFP (Non-Timber Forest Product)

Non-Timber Forest Product (NTFP), are the most important source of income, employment and food security for the rural households. These NTFPs attribute to 55 per cent of the total employment generated and are a source of livelihood to nearly 500 million people living in and around forests.

> Some of the NTFP gathered from the forest are broomshrubs, bamboo-shoots, wild edible plants and herbs, fruits, cinnamon, pepper, ginger etc. which have high economic value in the nearby urban markets, apart

> from household usage. Women play a most prominent role in collection, processing and sale of these products. The income raised by women in most of the times directly supplements the family food needs.

A large variety of Non-Timber Forest Products are used by the Khasis to supplement their daily food requirements. These include tubers, fruits, roots, wild edible plants, mushroom, bamboo shoot, creepers etc. A special kind of tuberous root locally called 'U Sohphlang' (*Flemingia Vestita*) is eaten raw.[5] The Khasis have a lot of wild plants which they use as their daily food and it is a natural quality of the Khasis to be able to differentiate between different wild plants. They can also distinguish between edible and poisonous mushrooms. It is also interesting to note that the Khasis generally use the prefix 'Ja' to name the wild variety of edible plants that are found in the woods. The reason for this could be that 'Ja' which literally means 'rice' is the staple food of the Khasis and so the use of these edible plants with the prefix 'Ja' was a supplement to rice specially amongst the poorer section of the people. Khongsit, who made an in-depth study on the various types and uses of forest produce' gives a list of 113 species of such plants and herbs that begin with the prefix 'Ja'.

Thus from an economic perspective, forest economy plays a central role in the livelihood strategies of Khasi rural households where women have played a significant role in collection, processing and even sale of forest products side by side in harmony with the domestic activities and thereby contributing directly to the household income.

It is a familiar sight to see women and children setting off into the woods to collect edible fruits and roots. A typical day out for an average Khasi village woman would be best described as follows:

> "She carries her baby on her back, climbing the hills she sets off for the woods with a *ja*-song (cooked rice

> packed in a leaf) salt and some dried fish (*ktung*). Going to the forest virtually takes her the whole day so besides collecting twigs and fuel wood and other forest products, she also spends the day washing clothes on the riverside in the foothills."

Needless to say, life has not been so easy for Khasi rural women. Their connection with forest resources is tradition bound and directly related to subsistence use. Thus, one cannot undermine the economic hardships faced by them in trying to utilize forests as supplementary sources of livelihood for their survival.

JHUM CULTIVATION OR THANG SHYRTI

Among the Khasis, this system of cultivation is known as "*Thang shyrti*" or "*Thang bun*". Essential features of *jhum* cultivation with special reference to Khasi Hills is as follows:

1. *Site selection:* Selection of sites for *jhum* practices is usually done by the individual owners of the land according to the needs of the family and family size. This is usually done before the month of December.
2. *Jungle cutting:* This operation is usually done in the months of December to January.
3. *Drying of Debris:* This operation follows just after the jungle is cleared and the debris is left to dry in the open.
4. *Burning:* Setting of fire to the dried debris is done from mid-February to March. This operation is done with care so as to avoid forest fires from spreading across to other hills, which were not meant for '*jhumming*'.
5. *Sowing/Planting:* Sowing and planting of various crops is done in an intimate mixture by dibbling. Upland paddy is the main crop grown in mixture with maize, millet, sorghum, tapioca, chillies, cotton, turmeric, pumpkin, etc.

6. Abandoning of Land after 3-5 years of cultivation and shifted to another site for repeating the same process.
7. The hutments of the village now remain at the same place in contrast to earlier days when the whole village shifted to new site.
8. *Cropping is done with minimum tillage:* No animals or large implements are used by the *jhum* cultivators for preparing land. The only implements used are the chopping knife, sickle, dibbling stick, spade and hoe.
9. There is practically no capital investment except labour and the seeds, which usually come from the household. *Jhum* cultivation has a chain of effects and after-effects leading to multifarious adverse conditions. The system causes far-reaching disturbances in the conditions of the soil leading to changes in the climate, ecological imbalance and the environmental degradation, besides the immediate results of fertility loss and low productivity of crops.
10. Firstly, the process of cutting and burning, *jhum* causes denudation of forests leading to two consequences, viz. ecological imbalance and elimination of the sources of water. Secondly, it causes soil erosion leading to silting up of rivers and streams which causes flood, on the other hand it affects fertility of the soil resulting in low productivity and pressure on land. Thirdly, the system of *jhum* is a primitive method with low technology involving much labour without subsidiary income. Lastly, it is a socially degrading system, detrimental to development programme and conservative in spirit and attitude of the *jhumias*.

Jhum Cultivation Area of Meghalaya

(i) Block-wise *Jhum* Cultivation area – Not Available.
(ii) District-wise *Jhum* Cultivation area as shown in the following table (based on the sample study conducted

by the Task Force Constitute by the State Government to study the problems of *Jhum* cultivation in the State):

Sl. No.	*Name of District*	*Annual Area under Jhum in Km² (Current year 2001)*
1.	East Khasi Hills	4.90
2.	West Khasi Hills	44.60
3.	Ri-Bhoi District	47.86
4.	Jaintia Hills	10.25
5.	East Garo Hills	92.61
6.	West Garo Hills	144.69
7.	South Garo Hills	62.41
	Total	**407.32**

Sl. No.	*Name of District*	*Annual Area affected by the Jhum for the last five years in Km²*
1.	East Khasi Hills	24.50
2.	West Khasi Hills	223.00
3.	Ri-Bhoi District	239.30
4.	Jaintia Hills	51.25
5.	East Garo Hills	463.05
6.	West Garo Hills	723.45
7.	South Garo Hills	312.05
	Total	**2036.60 Km²**

Bun Cultivation in Meghalaya

Shifting cultivation or *Jhumming* in Meghalaya is broadly classified into two categories based on the nature of the cultural operations: (1) Clear Felling *Jhumming* with least disturbance to the soil and (2) '*Bun*' Cultivation *Jhumming* involving disturbance to the soil. The second system of *jhumming*, locally known as '*Bun*' Cultivation, is mostly practiced by the *Jhummia* families of East Khasi Hills District, West Khasi Hills District and to some extent in Ri-Bhoi District and Jaintia Hills District.

In this system of *Jhumming*, the *jhummias* cut the shrubs and grasses (in the absence of forest cover) during the months of November/December and the cut materials are then laid in rows along the slope in bunds locally known as '*Bun*'. The soil surrounding the bunds/*Buns*, are then hoed and covered on top of these bunds/*Buns* during the months of December/January. Burning is done during January and planting is carried out from the end of February till March depending on the type of crops grown.

In this type of *jhumming*, the soil is very much disturbed and as a result, heavy soil erosion occurs during the monsoon periods leading to the depletion of soil fertility and exposing the sub-soil strata. The *jhummia* families are then left with no option but to apply manures and fertilizers to the crops grown on these bunds/*buns*.

Meghalaya with a total geographical area of 22,429 sq. kms. has a total of 2,64,960 number of families residing in 3,610 villages. As per the survey report conducted, the total number of *jhummia* families practicing *Bun* cultivation had been estimated to be at 10,262.

The District-wise Distribution of the *Jhummia* families is as follows:

Sl. No.	Districts	Area in Sq.kms.	No. of Jhummia Families	Families Practicing Bun Cultivation
1.	East Khasi Hills	2748	56,718	9355
2.	West Khasi Hills	5247	35,468	357
3.	Jaintia Hills	3819	34,425	Nil
4.	Ri-Bhoi	2448	24,220	556
5.	East Garo Hills	2603	33,289	Nil
6.	West Garo Hills	3714	59,386	Nil
7.	South Garo Hills	1850	21,457	Nil

East Khasi Hills: Bun cultivation is widely prevalent in the East Khasi Hills District. Majority of the farmers particularly the Mylliem C.D. Block, Mawphlang C.D. Block, Mawryngkneng C.D. Block and Mawkynrew C.D. Block, practice this type of cultivation. Potato, ginger, paddy, millet, maize, etc., are sown by the farmers as pure/mixed crop. Cultivation on the same plot is extended up to two years only and the plot is left fallow for a period of 3-5 years. Most of the farmers do not own the land but they cultivate the land on a long lease by paying an annual rent to the owners. Hence, it becomes a problem to take up any conservation measures as sometimes the lessee might agree but the owner refuses and *vice versa*. It had been estimated that about 13,755 families in the whole East Khasi Hills District practiced *Bun* cultivation.

West Khasi Hills District: In West Khasi Hills, the number of families involved in *Bun* cultivation had been estimated at 551.

Jaintia Hills District: The *jhummia* families involved in *Bun* cultivation had been estimated at 756.

Garo Hills: In the entire Garo Hills, there had been no practice of *Bun* cultivation.

REFRENCES

1. Vidyarthi, L.P. and Rai, B.K. 1976. *Tribal Culture of India*. New Delhi: Concept Publishing Company, pp.111-140
2. Gurdon, P.R.T. 1975. *The Khasis*. Delhi: Cosmo Publications, p. 158
3. Mawrie, H.O. 1981. *The Khasi Milieu*. New Delhi: Concept Publishing Company, p. 86
4. Uberoi Patricia. (ed). 1993. Family, Kinship and Marriage in India. Delhi : Oxford University Press, p.180
5. Gurdon, P.R.T. 1975. *The Khasis*. Delhi: Cosmo Publications, p. 51

Table 2.1 : District-wise Information of Villages and Families Dependency on '*Bun*' Cultivation

Sl. No.	*Name of District*	*Names of CD Blocks*	*Total No. of Villages*	*Total No. of Families practicing 'Bun' Cultivation*	*Jhummia Families*	*Total Population*	*Jhum area per Family in ha.*	*Persons per Family*
1	East Khasi Hills	1. Mylliem	97	13,150	3,075	70,607	1.00	5
		2. Mawphlang	158	7,873	5,590	46,685	1.50	6
		3. Mawryngkneng	62	6,326	2,564	35,914	0.50	6
		4. Mawkynrew	67	5,110	2,526	30,170	0.41	6
		5. Shella Bholaganj	191	7,736	Negligible	38,022	–	5
		6. Pynursla	152	9,404	Negligible	47,171	–	5
		7. Mawsynram	159	7,129	Negligible	38,194	–	5
		Total	**886**	**56,728**	**13,785**	**3,06,763**	**3.41**	**38**
2	West Khasi Hill	1. Nongstoin & Ranikor	240	7,852	Negligible	46,704	–	6
		2. Mairang	115	10,755	551	63,095	0.27	6
		3. Mawshynrut	261	7,069	Negligible	40,248	–	6
		4. Mawkyrwat	200	9,792	Negligible	55,771	–	6
		Total	**816**	**35,468**	**551**	**2,05,818**	**0.27**	**24**
3	Ri-Bhoi	1. Umling	264	9,717	Negligible	50,561	–	5
		2. Mawphlang	296	14,503	756	76,751	0.75	5
		Total	**260**	**24,220**	**756**	**1,27,312**	**0.75**	**10**

3 PARAMETERS OF FOREST USAGE IN KHASI SOCIETY

Khasi culture is filled with a rich splendour of ecological heritage. Every aspect of their culture, be it folklore, dance, music, food, religious activities etc. is a mosaic of interaction between people and nature. It would, therefore, be interesting to identify the domains or parameters within which forest operates in Khasi society which are enumerated under the following heads:

1. Forest Legends and Folklore

Forest myths and legends have played an important role in enriching the ecological history of societies around the world. Similarly, folklore is the hallmark of people's ethical and aesthetic norms and their values of life and is the index of the social, cultural and emotional evolution of that society. Folklore represents the archaic thought of mankind, their sense of human values and their worldview. It is a mirror through which one can perceive the past cultural and historical landscape of a people. Dr. Suniti Kumar Chatterjee called folklore "*Lokayana*" that signifies a way of life of a community (*Loka* - community, *Yana* - way of life).

The Khasis have maintained a close symbiotic relationship with environment since time immemorial and their ethno-cultural traits have been greatly influenced by the natural surroundings. A well-known Khasi legend centres on the belief in "*U Diengiei*", a giant tree that is very popular among them. According to this legend there was a very tall and gigantic tree at Lum Diengiei with its branches spread far and wide that covered the sun overshadowing the earth. The whole world became dark and damp and the people, deprived of the warmth of the sun and light suffered from ill- health, disease and death. So they held their village council meetings and decided to cut down the tree, and ultimately it was only after they had felled the tree that they could enjoy health, peace and happiness.[1] This folktale throws ample light on the attitude and perception of the ancient Khasis towards tree and forest. They considered forest as the home of Gods and evil spirits, as something dreadful and looked them with a sense of awe and reverence.

The Khasi folklore and legends, "*Khanatang bad Puriskam*" are mostly woven around the various forces of nature such as the hills and vales, rocks and caves, the flora and fauna. These elements of nature are personified in the legends as the mother and son, husband and wife and friend and foe according to their natural behaviours, their love, hate, jealousy, pride and vanity which are projected out before the listeners with the sole purpose of teaching moral and spiritual values. To give a few examples out of many, in the folktale of "*U Klew bad ka Sngi*" (The Peacock and the Sun), the peacock has been personified as the husband of the sun. Both of them lived happily in the sky. One fine morning the peacock saw a beautiful mustard field in full bloom on earth below.

He thought that it was the most beautiful maiden he had ever seen. Thereupon, he decided to fly down to earth and meet her. The sun, his wife, begged him not to go leaving her behind, but that did not deter him. But on descending on the earth he could see that the beautiful virgin was nothing but a mere field of mustard plants. The peacock lamented for his silly mistake and shed his tears all upon his feathers, which created those spots that the peacock still carries on his wings. This story gives the moral lesson of conjugal fidelity between husband and wife.

Another famous legend is about the use of betel nut, betel leaf and tobacco, which is an essential item among the Khasi. The story is about a poor couple "U Shing" and his wife "Ka

Lak" who had a very intimate well to do friend by the name of "U Nik Mahajon". Whenever the couple visited their friend's house, they were welcomed with honour and were treated to sumptuous meals. However, one day when U Nik Mahajon visited the couple, they were taken by surprise not to find anything in the house to offer to their guest. "Ka Lak" went round the neighbourhood begging for some food but came back empty handed. Overcome by shame and desperation, the couple took a knife and killed themselves. When U Nik Mahajon found them dead in the kitchen and understood the cause for the suicide, he too took the same knife and ended his life in the same manner.

It so happened that a thief entered the house that night and seeing the three dead bodies, understood that he would be blamed for this so in utter desperation, he too ended his own life. When the people realized this sad event, they begged God to give them a simpler way of welcoming friends. The ancient Khasis have compared these three people to the three most valued things in the household, namely, the betel nut, leaf, lime and tobacco. The betel nut stands for the rich friend, the betel leaf and the lime to the couple and the tobacco to the thief. This legend accounts for the Khasi way of greeting a guest no matter how poor or rich they may be, it has been a norm of hospitality to offer *kwai* (betel nut, leaf and lime) to welcome friends and guests into their homes.

2. Forest for Shelter

Every Khasi believes that their beautiful land of "*U Hynniewtrep*" (seven huts) "*Hynniewskum*" (seven nests) is a gift from God almighty. This divine belief of the origin of the Khasis gives us an idea of the use of thatch and grass by the ancient Khasis for building houses. The houses of the people are cleaner than might be supposed after taking into consideration the dirtiness of the clothes and persons of those who inhabit them. They are, as a rule, substantial thatched cottages with plank or stonewalls and rose on a plinth some 2 to 3 ft. from the ground. The only window is a small opening on one side of the house, which admits but a dim light into the smoke-begrimed interior. The beams are so low that it is impossible for a person of ordinary stature to stand erect within.

The fire is always burning on an earthen or stone hearth in the centre. There is no chimney, the smoke finding its exit as best it can. The firewood is placed to dry on a swinging frame above the hearth.[2] It was considered a taboo *'sang'* to use iron nails while constructing a Khasi house and in olden days, only a certain kind of timber was used for the fender, which surrounds the hearth. Hard wood was preferred amongst which Jackfruit, Champa, *Albizzia odoratisima*, *Euginia tetragona* and different species of Oak were used. The Khasis considered it a taboo to use *Makria* Sal in any part of the house.[3]

The houses of the Pnar-Wars are peculiar. The roof, which is thatched with the leaves of a palm called "*U Tynriew*", is hog-backed and the leaves come down almost to the ground.[4] The Bhoi and Lyngam houses are practically similar and they are generally built on fairly high platforms of bamboo, which are frequently 30 to 40 ft. in length. A particular species of tree "*Ka Latar*" (*Verbaneceae; Rubella callicarpum*) grown abundantly in the Bhoi and War region grows as high as 70 to 80 ft. Its bark is very strong and can be stripped out easily from stem to the branches without breaking it. This bark is used since time immemorial in tying up the wooden poles while constructing a house.

3. Forest for Household Utensils and Furniture

As in the case of houses, so with reference to furniture the influence of civilization shows many changes with regard to the use of furniture and household utensils.

The furniture of the kitchen is simple with the humble wooden stool (*lyngknot*) to sit upon around the fire. Above the hearth is slung by ropes of cane a swinging wooden framework blackened with the smoke of years, upon which are spread the faggots of resinous fir-wood used for kindling the fire. Above this is again a wooden framework fixed on the beams of the house, upon which all sorts of odds and ends are kept. Around the fire are to be seen small wooden stools upon which the members of the household sit.

Up-to-date Khasis have cane chairs, but the women of the family, true to the conservative instincts of the sex, prefer the humble stool to sit upon. Well-to-do Khasis now-a-days have in addition to the ordinary cooking vessels made of iron and earthenware, a number of brass utensils. The ordinary cultivator uses a water pot made from a gourd hollowed out for keeping water and liquor in and drinks from a bamboo cylinder.

In the sleeping rooms of the well to do there are wooden beds with mattresses and sheets and pillows, clothes being hung upon clothes racks. The ordinary cultivator and his wife sleep on mats made of plaited bamboo, which are spread on the bare boards of the house. There are various kinds of mats (*shylliah*) to be met with in the Khasi houses made of plaited cane, of a kind of reed and of plaited bamboo. The best kind of mat is prepared from cane. In all Khasi houses are to be seen "*ki knup*" or rain shields of different sizes and sometimes of somewhat different shapes.

Baskets of different shapes and sizes (*khoh*), which are carried on the back, slung across the forehead by a head-strap, are commonly used.

The ones that are conical in shape tapering at the bottom are generally used with a bamboo cover to protect the contents of the basket from rain.[5] Paddy is husked in a wooden mortar by means of a heavy wooden pestle.

Sometimes a bamboo sieve is used for sifting the husked rice, a winnowing fan being applied to separate the husk. The clean rice is exposed to the sun in a bamboo tray.

It is interesting to note that the most widely used household items are made out of bamboo. Betel leaves (*tympew*) are kept in a bamboo tube and tobacco leaves in a smaller one.

4. Forest for Musical Instruments

The Khasis love dances, music and songs. From time immemorial, the Khasis have their own indigenous musical instruments, which consists of different kinds of drums, pipes, harps and cymbals. The musical instruments are of different types, sizes and styles and are locally made which allow the artistic skill of the Khasi. The different types of musical instruments are:

1. The Drums :
   (a) '*Ka bom ka nakra bad tasar*' or the big drum.
   (b) '*Ka ksing bom*' or '*sing nakra*' or the smaller drum.
   (c) '*Ka ksing kynthei*' or the female drum.
   (d) '*Ka Ksing shynrang*' or the male drum.
   (e) '*Ka padiah bad ka ksing dingphong*' are smaller drums.
2. Musical Instruments: Some of the stringed instruments are '*ka duitara*', '*ka marynthing*', '*ka maryngod*'.
3. Blowing Instruments:
   (a) '*Ka tangmuri ne Ka Muhuri*'
   (b) '*Ka Sharati*'
   (c) '*Ka besli*'
   (d) '*Ka mieng*'
   (e) '*Ka shawiang*'
   (f) '*Ka tanglod*'
   (g) '*Ka put sla*'

All these blowing instruments are made of bamboo except '*Ka put sla*'.[6] Khasi drums are nearly always made of wood, not of metal or earthenware. '*Ka Padiah*' is a small drum with a handle made of wood while '*Ka Ksing*' is a cylindrically shaped drum and '*Ka nakra*' is a large kettledrum made of wood having the head covered with deerskin. '*Ka duitara*' is a guitar with

muga silk strings, which is played with a little wooden key held in the hand. ***'Ka tangmuri'*** is a wooden pipe, which is played like a flageolet. The Khasis also play a Jew's harp (***ka mieng***), which is made of bamboo.[7]

Thus we find that the Khasis make an extensive use of bamboo and wood in their indigenous musical instruments.

5. Forest for Weaving and Dying

The Khasis learnt how to depict various designs and colours in their clothing from nature. They are well acquainted with the art of weaving.

A great many number of weaver families were seen by Gurdon in Khyrwang villages of Synteng, Mynso and Sutnga. The Khyrwangs weave special pattern of cotton and silk cloth with stripped red and white. Before the British came, this industry was considerable. The Census conducted before 1907 gives the number of weavers in Khasi Jaintia as 533. The Khasis of Bhoi weave cotton and dye it with leaves of a plant called ***'U Nob'*** for black colour. They also boil the coloured thread in the leaves of a tree called ***'Ka Lakhynroh'*** (***Symplocaceae; Symplocus glomerata***) to make the colour a lasting one. They also use the bark of the tree called ***'Dieng Pyrshit'*** (***Eurya accuminata latifolia***) for dying thread. It gives a yellow colour.

There is a village Umrasun in Bhoi area where Khasis are still weaving their clothes with various designs and colours. The special cloths they make are called *'Phali'*. In this cloth they depict designs of trees, bamboos, flowers, animals and birds with threads already dyed in various colours obtained from lac or from leaves and barks of trees. They also observe a festival every year where they only wear clothes woven by them.

The festival is an indication of how the people of the place give importance to their culture and art and their expertise in making beautiful clothes.

Rearing of Eri Silk worm (***khñiang ryndia***) is an ancient art known to Khasis. They use a tree called ***'Ka Lakynjor'***

(*Bignonaceae; Oxyllum indica*) as feed for the silkworm. They also cultivate '*Larynda*' (castor plant) for this purpose .[8]

The Khasis also carry out lac culture by rearing insect on the '*Sohphyrnu* tree'. They tie the insects on this tree where they eat and grow up and increase in number. They collect lac in the month of October. Another type of tree called '*Ka Jrisim*' in Bhoi is also used for rearing lac insect. Lac is cultured till today in Nongstoin areas in a village known as '*Umsohpieng*'. They use the tree named '*dieng Risim*' in these areas. During the lean season the lac cultivators preserve lac insect on the trees called '*U toh Laha*' (*Popilianceae; Cajanus indica*) as seed until the time for cultivation arrives. This tree is small about 8 to 10 ft. tall with green barks and grows well in Bhoi. During winter, the insects are kept on the '*Toh Laha Tree*' then are transferred to Diengsohphyrnu or Jrisim or Diengrai for cultivation.

A particular tree called '*Ka Dieng Sohtung*' (*Aralia* Sp.; *Araliaceae*) has black coloured leaves and the Khasis of yore used theses leaves for dying threads for making the '*jymphong*' or sleeveless coat worn by men.

Rev. W.M. Jenkins in his book entitled *Life and Work in Khasia*, writes in 1841, "the men wearing simply a fringed jacket roughly woven of hemp (cotton) just reaching the thighs and with the arms bare...".

Besides these trees the following species of trees are also used as dyes:

(a) *Ka Nuli* (*Strobilanthes secundus*) – brilliant black colour
(b) *Ka Pantaro* (*Strobilanthes*) – brilliant red colour
(c) *Ka Dieng Mitang* – red colour of different shades.

6. Forest for Weaponry

The weapons of the Khasis are swords, spears, bows and arrows and a circular shield, which was used formerly for purposes of defence.[9] It is surprising that in the Khasi sword, the handle is never made of wood or bone or of anything except iron or steel, the result being that the sword is most awkward to hold and could never have been of much use as a weapon of offence.

The Khasi weapon par excellence is the bow. Archery may be styled as the Khasi national game.[10] The Khasi bow '*Ka ryntieh*' is made of bamboo and is used mostly for hunting purposes. The bowstring is of split bamboo and the bamboos that are used are of 3 types: (a) '*U spit*', (b) '*U shken*' and (c) '*U siej-lieh*'.

The Khasi arrow '*Khnam*' are generally of two types: (a) The plain-headed (*sop*); (b) The barbed-headed (*ki pliang*). Both types are made of bamboo. The feathers of birds like vultures, geese, cranes, cormorants and hornbills are used for arrows.

7. Forest in Khasi Rituals and Ceremonies

Rituals abound in Khasi religion and culture. In the words of H.O. Mawrie, *"Ka Kolshor bad ka niam ki long kiba la ngam ha ki thied snam jong ngi kum ka jaitbynriew bad ban bret ia ki ka long kumba patar da lade ia lade."* ("Rituals are a part and parcel of our culture. They have embedded their roots deep down in our flesh and blood and to think of mankind to throw away either of them is to tear oneself apart.") There are rituals pertaining to three important stages in one's life:

(1) Naming ceremony (*ka jer ka thoh*)
(2) Marriage (*poikha-poiman*)
(3) Death (*niam ïap*)

(1) Naming Ceremony

The following are some instances of the use of forest products during the birth ceremony:

(a) When the child is born, a sharp splinter of bamboo cuts the umbilical cord. No knife can be used on this occasion.

(b) When the umbilical cord, after being tied falls off, a ritual is performed by offering worship to certain water deities '*Ka blei sam-um*' and also to forest spirit' '*U 'suid bri*' or "*U 'suid khlaw*'.
(c) For the naming ceremony, the pounded rice flour is placed on a bamboo winnower called '*U prah.*'
(d) A plantain leaf is used to place five pieces of '*Kha piah*' or dried fish.
(e) Liquor is placed in a gourd (*klong*).

(2) Marriage Ceremony

A simple wedding ceremony of the Khasi would include the exchange of distilled liquor from two gourds (*klong*) which are mixed together. The priest then says a prayer of blessing over the couple and pours the entire liquor on to the three '*khapiah*' or dry fish. These are then placed in a container and preserved over the hearth.

(3) Death Ceremony

The following instances of the use of forest products are evident in death ceremonies of the Khasis:

(a) The dead body is laid on a mat (*japung*) made of bamboo.
(b) A small bamboo basket (*ka shang*) is hung up over the head of the corpse.
(c) Sometimes the body is placed in a coffin, which is laid on a bamboo bier (*ka krong*).
(d) As the funeral party sets out to the bone repository (*mawshieng*), one person in front strews a line of route leaves of the tree known by the Khasis as '*dieng shit*'. If any stream is to be crossed, a rough bridge is made of branches and grass. This trail of leaves and the bridges are intended to guide the spirit of the deceased to the cairn.

8. Forest for Agriculture

Agriculture has been extensively carried out as an important means of subsistence especially cultivation of highland rice or dry cultivation and lowland rice or wet cultivation. Besides rice, the cultivation of potato, orange, betel nut and ***paan*** are also carried out. Agricultural implements used by the Khasis in cultivation include:

- A large hoe (***mohkhiew heh***)
- An axe for felling trees (***u sdie***)
- A large dao for felling trees (***ka wait lyngam***)
- Two kinds of bill-hooks (***ka wait prat*** and ***ka wait khmut***)
- A sickel (***ka rashi***)
- A harrow (***ka iuh moi***)

Gurdon classifies the agricultural lands of the Khasis into: (a) Forest lands; (b) Wet paddy lands called '***hali***' or '***pynthor***' and (c) homestead land (***ka dew kper***).

It is generally in the forestlands where trees are cleared by '***jhumming***' i.e., by burning the felled trees that are then left as wood ashes till the time comes for the seeds to be sown. There is a well-known saying among the Khasi farmers relating to planting of trees—"***Thung dieng ne bet symbai haba ngen u bnai, ym haba shai u bnai...***". "Plant trees or sow seeds not when the moon is waxing but when it is on the wane."

9. Forest for Food

A large variety of Non-Timber-Forest Products are used by the Khasis to supplement their daily food requirements. These include tubers, fruits, roots, wild edible plants, mushroom, bamboo shoot, creepers etc. A special kind of tuberous root locally called '*U sohphlang*' (***Flemingia vestita***) is eaten raw (Gurdon, 1975:51). The Khasis have a lot of wild plants which they use as their daily food and it is a natural quality of the

Khasis to be able to differentiate between different wild plants. They can also distinguish between edible and poisonous mushrooms. The Khasis know of a wide variety of mushrooms, each of which they call by name. A trip into the woods and forests to collect vegetables and mushrooms is something they love and do regularly.[11]

It is also interesting to note that the Khasis generally use the prefix '*Ja*' to name the wild variety of edible plants that are found in the woods. The reason for this could be that '*Ja*' which literally means 'rice' is the staple food of the Khasis and so the use of these edible plants with the prefix '*Ja*' was a supplement to rice specially amongst the poorer section of the people. Khongsit, who made an indepth study on the various types and uses of forest produce with the prefix '*Ja*' gives a list of 113 species of such plants and herbs. The list of such plants and herbs is given in Appendix-I.

10. Forest as Woodcrafts and Bamboo Crafts

From a historical retrospective, the traditional woodcraft and bamboo craft, which were in existence since the long centuries past, are still in use till today.[12] The following is a list of several articles of daily use made from cane and bamboo :

- *(a)* *Trap* or *Japi* (a container for serving as a package used for travelling)
- *(b)* *Khoh* (a conical structure with a seat provided, used for carrying sick persons or travellers)
- *(c)* *Knup* (used as a cap by women to protect oneself from the hot sun and rain)
- *(d)* *Pdung* and *Prah* (winnowing fans and trays)
- *(e)* *Shang* (baskets)
- *(f)* *Mula* (stools made of cane slips)

Bamboo or '*siej*' as it is locally called is of multifarious use. Khongsit in his book *Hangne Tang ïa u Siej*, gives the names of

43 species of bamboo that are locally grown and used for different purposes by the Khasis. The list of such species has been provided in Appendix-II.

Bamboo is modelled into several crafts, baskets and other articles such as fishing rods, water or irrigation pipes, huts, ***mechangs*** or platforms, bridges, decorative gates, chairs, toys, furniture, containers, water vessels etc. Mats are also woven out of special bamboo called '*siej lieh*'. Thus, one can say that there was once a widespread bamboo culture.[13]

Woodcraft finds expression in the handles of hoes, knives, daggers, *daos* and sometimes spears. An important item used in Khasi kitchens till today is the mortar and pestle or '*U thlong*' and '*synrei*' made of wood for pounding.

11. Forest for Fruits

Meghalaya is rich in fruit bearing trees which grow wild around the hills and dales of the State. Most of these wild fruits not only serve as natural food for the birds and animals but also are edible to human beings. They are delicious and health giving with full of vitamins and minerals much needed for our body. Some of them possess medicinal values. According to Botanists there are 136 different varieties of fruits found in five agro-climatic zones of Meghalaya.

The rich diversity of the flora of the region is attributable to both natural selection and to some extent domestication. While most of the fruits are used for local consumption some of the wild fruits of the state have very high commercial potential due to three unique taste and hardy nature. The local Khasi people eat different parts of the fruits such as the pulp, the seed and the juice depending on their qualities. Some fruits are eaten raw, some are boiled and sliced and still some others are processed into pickles and beverages.

In the following table some of the major fruits are shown in details with their local names, botanical names, harvesting seasons and their usages:

Table 3.1 : List of major fruits

Sl. No.	*Local Name*	*Botanical Name*	*Season*	*Usages*
1	*Sohthri*	*Calamus fleribundus*	Mar/Apr	Delicious fruit. Edible part is fruit pulp
2	*Sohsiah*	*Rubus olliplicus*	Feb/Mar	Tasty edible raspberry
3	*Sohshang*	*Elaegnus conferta khasiana*	Mar/May	Sour in taste, used for pickle
4	*Sohphie Nam*	*Myrica nagi*	Apr/Jul	Tastiest wild fruit. Bark is used for medicine
5	*Sohphie Bah*	*Myrica esculenta*	Apr/Jul	Sour in taste, used for pickle
6	*Sohliang*	*Gynocardia odorata*	Jan/Mar	Seeds are first boiled and sliced to eat. Tree has medicinal value.
7	*Sohram-dieng*	*Baccauria sapida*	Jun/Jul	Delicious, edible part is juice.
8	*Sohmluh*	*Haccartia cataphraeta*	Aug/Oct	Edible fruit. Wood is used for agricultural tools.
9	*Sohïong*	*Prunus nepalensis*	Aug/Oct	Delicious fruit, used for making jam, squashes and wine.
10	*Sohmad*	*Citrus medica*	August	Edible fruit. The plant is used for medicine.
11	*Sohmang-kariang*	*Citus sinensis*	Nov/Jan	Edible fruit.

12. Forest for Apiculture

Apiculture or bee-keeping is an age-old tradition of the Khasis. The forests of Khasi Hills abound in many varieties of wild bees which are known to Khasis about their nature, habits and productive quality. Commonly preferred species in Khasi Hills is the smaller variety that is amenable to home environment and of lesser ferocity in nature. It is a common site in Khasi rural areas to see bee-hives reared in hollow logs of wood or ordinary wooden boxes hung in the corner of cattle sheds or store houses. Now-a-days they also use improved variety of bee-hive boxes obtained from the Industries Department of the Government.

Due to abundance of nectar bearing flowers in and around the forests, bee-keeping industry has proved to be a good source of income for many Khasi families. One apiarist told the investigator that he has three bee colonies from which he harvests 3 to 4 kg. of honey from each hive at 3 to 4 months interval. He sells pure honey at Rs.150.00 per kg. in the market.

Apart from many natural products like timber, sandstone, limestone and citrus fruits, honey is also an important product they sell and which forms as a subsidiary source of income to the Khasi farmers in addition to the income from agriculture. There are basically four types of bee-hives in Meghalaya, viz. wooden log type, rock type, cement block type and the recent Newton's bee-hive.

A study conducted by ICAR Research Complex for NEH Region reveals that due to destruction of forests in the hilly state of Meghalaya for cultivation and other purposes, clearing the land for raising grasses for grazing etc. have been some of the reasons for reduction in the number of beekeepers, as the bee pasturage is becoming less. However, bee-keeping is still widely practised by the Khasis. As one apiarist in Cherrapunjee said "selling honeybees is a taboo in Khasis society. The honeybee is a taboo in Khasis society. The honeybee, we consider it as the mother. Do you sell your mother? We cannot fix price for honeybees. If we sell them, something bad will happen in seller's family."

13. Forest for Medicine

The Khasis are known for their unique knowledge about plants wealth and herbals drugs in curing diseases. The origin of Khasi system of medicine is not known, as Khasi folklore and legend are silent about its origin. But the psychological, social and cultural contribution to this system is very prominent.

Since time immemorial the folk medicine has been evolved, practised and developed and even today it has an enormous resource potential for the care and management of health problems. The traditional system of medicine of the Khasis, unlike that of other communities of India, is not looked down upon as primitive and crude way of treatment, but majority of the rural population in Khasi Hills still rely on this for their primary health care needs. In this case one cannot deny that the socio-cultural and psychological forces play a large part in determining the causes, nature and means of counteracting illness. Most of the diseases and social disabilities arise from the social conditions, unhealthy lifestyle, food-habits and high-risk behaviour of the community. The prevalence of endemic and racial diseases is the example of this. Mr. William C. Cockerham writes – "Health is, therefore, not simply a matter of biology but involves a number of factors that are social, cultural, political and economic in nature".

Nearly 400 B.C. ago, Hippocrates, the Greek Physician, pointed out that human well-being is influenced by the totality of environmental factors, living habits or lifestyle, climate, topography of the land and the quality of air, water and food.

It is for this reason that forest plays a great role in determining the problems and management of health of a community. The Khasi hills are abounding in large varieties of medicinal plants and herbs.

Its climate, rainfall, soil condition and topography contribute to the growth of dark forests, shrubs and thickets, which are the ideal home to valuable medicinal plants. Many of these plants, which are often considered as weeds, are very important for their medicinal properties.

Table 3.2 shows the major plants and herbs available in Khasi hills and the diseases treated by those plants.

14. Forests as Sacred Abodes

Preservation of forests as sacred groves has been existent since time immemorial amongst the Khasis. People are mostly governed by their belief systems in conserving these forests. The existence of "*U Ryngkew U Basa*" or "the guardian spirit" in these forests is a belief that has existed amongst the Khasis since

Table 3.2 : Major Plants and Herbs in Khasi Hills

Sl. No.	*Scientific Name*	*Local Name*	*Parts Used*	*Diseases Treated*
1.	*Andrographis paniculata*	*Kynbat jyrngam*	Roots	Rheumatic pains, Anti-helmintic
2.	Ageratum conyzoides	Kynbat *blumyngai*	Leaves	Cuts, Bleeding, Antidote for snakebite.
3.	*Artemisia nilagirica*	*Khel bijak*	Leaves	Asthma, Brain diseases, Sores.
4.	Centela asiatica	Kynbat Moina/ *Khleiñ Syiar*	Leaves & roots	Dysentery, Blood pressure, Skin diseases
5.	*Flemingia vestita*	*Sohphlang*	Root bank	Tape worms and worms eradication
6.	*Mimosa pudica*	*Kynbat samthiah*	Leaves, roots & stems	Piles, Hydrocele, Scorpion sting.
7.	*Eupatorium odoratum*	*Krah-lynroh*	Leaf	Bleeding and Dysentery.
8.	*Galinsoga parviflora*	*Tiew-lien*	Leaves	Bleeding and Insect sting.
9.	*Drymaria cordata*	*Thei phelwang*	Whole plant	Diarrhoea, Vomiting, Urinary problem, antidote for snakebite.
10.	*Imaptiens racemosa*		Leaves & roots	Rheumatic pains.
11.	*Nepethes khasiana*	*Tiew rakot*	Pitcher	Ear disease and cholera.
12.	*Oxalis corniculata*	*Soh-dkhiew*	Leaves	Cough, snakebite, dysentery.
13.	*Potentila fulgens*	*Lyngniang-bru*	Whole plant	Colic pain, spasmodic trouble, pyorrhoea.
14.	*Plantago major*	*Shkor Blang*	Leaves & roots	Bleeding injuries/wounds
15.	*Panax pseudoginseng*	*Kynbat syieng jinseng*	Roots	Aphrodisiac, Hypothermia, Asthma, Rheumatism.
16.	*Solanum xanthocarpum*	*Dieng-phydok bakthang*	Roots & fruits	Flatulence, Threadworm, Tuberculosis.
17.	*Taxus bacata*	*Sohblei*	Leaves	Aphrodisiac, Epilepsy and Irregular menstruation.
18.	Viscum articulatum	Mangkariang *khlem sla*	Whole plant	Snake bite, wounds.
19.	*Zinger officinalis*	*Sying*	Rhizoma	Cough, Rheumatism.
20.	*Mikania micrantha*	*Momoshathap*	*Leaves*	Stomach trouble.
21.	*Polygonum orientale*	*Agasom*	*Leaves*	Severe headache.
22.	*Uraria crinita*	*Dieng kharia*	*Roots*	High fevers.
23.	*Chenopodium* ambroisioides	*Slah sam*	*Plant*	Nervous tension.
24.	*Emilia sonchifolia*	*Soh Byshet*	Leaf juice	Eye problems.
25.	Musa sapientum	Ka Kait	*Root, fruit,* stem	Dysentery, Diarrhoea, Boil, Worms.

time immemorial. The 'guardian spirit', according to them, resides in the forest and takes care of the village community and protects them from sickness, pain, invasion by enemies, etc. Therefore, destroying or cutting of trees, grass etc. from these groves is considered to be against the wish of *U Ryngkew U Basa* and, therefore, people are afraid of these spirits.[14]

"*Law Kyntang*" as they are generally known are also known by various names such as "*Law Lyngdoh*" or "*Law Niam*". These forests are set aside for religious purposes and are managed by the Lyngdoh (a religious priest) or any other person to whom the religious ceremonies for the particular locality are entrusted. Till today, these sacred groves are held in high esteem and every now and then religious ceremonies including worship of forest deities, dances and rituals are regularly performed, by the '*Lyngdoh*' together with the villagers inside the grove. Mention may be made of the sacred grove at Pahampdem village located at Ri Bhoi district which is popularly known by the local people as '*U Lum Mawker*' or '*U Lum Umphar*'. The grove is the biggest recorded sacred grove in the state with an area of 900 ha.

This grove belongs to the '*Lyngdoh Syntiew*' clan and so management of the grove is left to the clan council. Besides its religious significance, these groves serve as a natural habitat for many rare species of flora and fauna. The importance of sacred groves in biodiversity conservation has also been recognised in recent times. In Meghalaya, sacred groves belong either to private owners or to clans and communities. As such, the legal status accorded to these groves is in accordance with the acts of the respective District Councils of Khasi, Jaintia and Garo Hills.

The United Khasi-Jaintia Hills Autonomous District (Management and Control of Forests) Act, 1958, also referred to as Act 1 of 1958 is the principal Act for the management and control of the forests in the autonomous district area.[15] This act was later appended with the United Khasi-Jaintia Hills Autonomous District Rules or Rules 1960. According to the Rules 1960, all the private forests including sacred groves (*Law Lyngdoh*, *Law Kyntang* and *Law Niam*) in the area of the District

Council are to be registered with the Chief Forest Officer mentioning the home addresses of with the boundaries and such other particulars of the forests as may be required. No timber or forest produce from *Law Kyntang*, *Law Lyngdoh* and *Law Niam* are allowed to be felled or removed except for purposes in connection with religious functions or ceremonies recognised and sanctioned by the *Lyngdoh* (religious head) and other persons in accordance with Section 4(b) (Section 9 of the Act 1958).[16]

Table 3.3 : Locations and Estimated Area of Sacred Forests in East Khasi Hills, West Khasi Hills, Ri Bhoi, Jaintia Hills, West Garo Hills and East Garo Hills Districts of Meghalaya

Sl. No.	*Names of the Groves*	*Distance from Shillong (km)*	*Area (ha)*	*Village*	*Controlling Authority (Syiemship/ Dolloiship/ Nokmaship etc.)*
JAINTIA HILLS					
1.	Blai Law	85	0.01	Raliang	Raliang Dolloiship
2.	Poh Puja Ko Patti	74	4		Raliang Dolloiship
3.	Poh Moorang	90	20	Raliang	Raliang Dolloiship
4.	Ka Pun Lyngdoh	85	15	Raliang	Raliang Dolloiship
5.	Khlaw Byrsan	80	50	Raliang	Raliang Dolloiship
6.	Poh Lyngdoh	74	30	Shangpung	Shangpung Dolloiship
7.	Law Kyntang	74	400	Shangpung	Shangpung Dolloiship
8.	Khlaw Blai	105	15	Dien Shynrum	Rymbai Dolloiship
9.	Khloo Paiu Ram Pyrthai	60	150	Panaliar	Jowai Dolloiship
10.	Trepale Jowai	60	70	Panaliar	Jowai Dolloiship
11.	Khloo Lyngdoh	60	15	Panaliar	Jowai Dolloiship
12.	Mokhain Sacred Grove	60	45	Khimmusiang	Jowai Dolloiship
13.	Dpepat Myndihati	110	15	Myndhihati	Sutnga Dolloiship
14.	Lumtiniang Mokalaw Syndai	115	25	Syndai	Satpator Dolloiship

Table 3.3 : *(Contd...)*

RI BHOI					
15	Pahampdem	55	900	Pahampdem	Raid Umsaw-Nongkharai
16	Nonglyngdoh	55	90	Nongkhrah	Nongpoh Sirdarship
17	Sohpetbneng Sacred Grove	40	90	Nongkhrah	Nongpoh Sirdarship
EAST KHASI HILLS					
18.	Law Lyngdoh	25	75	Mawphlang	Mawphlang Lyndohship
19.	Law Lyngdoh Nongkrem	14	6	Smit	Khyrim Syiemship
20.	Lum Shillong	8	7	Laitkor	Khyrjm Syiemship
21.	Law Kyntang	53	50	Khlieh Shnong	Sohra Syiemship
22.	Law Adong	53	90	Khlieh Shnong	Sohra Syiemship
23.	Khlaw Ram Jadong	55	50	Mawsmai	Mawsmai Syiemship
24.	Law Blei Bah	55	120	Mawsmai	Mawsmai Syiemship
25.	Mawlong Syiem	55	120	Mawsmai	Mawsmai Syiemship
26.	Pom Shandi Syiemship	55	80	Mawsmai	M a w s m a i
27.	Law Adong	55	400	Mawsmai	Mawsmai Syiemship
28.	Law Suidnoh	45	80	Laitryngew	Sohra Syiemship
29.	Law-u-Niang	45	10	Laitryngew	Sohra Syiemship
30.	Madan Jadu	45	5	Laitryngew	Sohra Syiemship
31.	Law-ar-Liang	38	25	Khadar Blang	Khyrim Syiemship
32.	Lum Diengjri	75	25	Khadar Shnong	Sohra Syiemship
33.	Mawmang Sacred Grove	60	15	KhadarShnong	Sohra Syiemship
34.	Wahkhen Sacred Grove	35	10	Khadar Blang	Khyrim Syiemship
35.	Law Lieng	42	20	Sohra Rim	Khatsawphra Syiemship
36.	Law Mawsaptur	42	50	Sohra Rim	Sohra Syiemship
37.	Law Dymmiew	42	200	Sohra Rim	Sohra Syiemship
38.	Law Nongshim	43	5	Mawmih	Sohra Syiemship
39.	Mawsawa	55	50	Mawmluh	Sohra Syiemship
40.	Mawryot	62	40	Wahlong	Wahlong Sirdarship
41.	Niangdoh	62	30	Wahlong	Wahlong Sirdarship
42.	Rijaw	62	35	Wahlong	Wahlong Sirdarship
43.	Umtong	63	400	Umwai	Umwai Sirdarship
44.	Diengkain	63	400	Umwai	Umwai Sirdarship
45.	Mawthong	63	600	Umwai	Umwai Sirdarship
46.	Maw Kyrngah	63	1200	Umwai	Umwai Sirdarship
47.	Kynsang	65	150	Mawlong	Mawlong Sirdarship
48.	Umthri	65	80	Mawlong	Mawlong Sirdarship

Table 3.3 : *(Contd...)*

49.	Umkatait	65	100	Mawlong	Mawlong Sirdarship
50.	Ulaw Lyngdoh	91	90	Nonglyngkien	Maharam Syiemship
51.	Ulum Sanglia	92	45	Nonglyngkien	Maharam Syiemship
52.	Ulaw Blei	90	55	Nonglyngkien	Maharam Syiemship
53.	Law Lyngdoh	80	200	Nonglang	Maharam Syiemship
54.	Law Kyntang	80	300	Mawlangwiar	Maharam Syiemship
55.	Law Kyntang	75	100	Mawten	Maharam Syiemship
56.	Law Lyngdoh	70	400	Rangmaw	Maharam Syiemship
57.	Law Kyntang	90	100	Mawthawiaw	Maharam Syiemship
58.	Nongsynrih Sacred Grove	92	100	Nongsynrih	Maharam Syiemship
59.	Law Lyngdoh	75	50	Nonglait	Maharam Syiemship
60.	Law Adong Lyngdoh Mawlong	43	200	Mawlong	Nongkhlaw Syiemship
61.	Kyllai Lyngngum	104	80	Marian	Nobosohphoh Syiemship
62.	Lyngdoh Mawnai Sacred Grove	104	80	Mawnai	Nobosohphoh Syiemship

Uses of Certain Species of Trees

1. Ka Kain (Succedaneae)

This is a big tree with large fruits, which the birds are very fond of. It produces to the one who touches it, itching and ulcers. Timber from this tree is used for making a musical instrument called '*Duitara*' because it is light in weight and gives out sweet tune by its soft and vibrating quality. When the makers of the *duitara* go out in the woods to cut the tree, they utter a few words to please the tree spirits.

They say, "*Hey nga ibha ia pha*", which means "Oh! I love you", this is done before they even touch the tree because they believe that if they say so the tree will not produce itching in their bodies.

2. Ka Dieng Jri (Urticeceae; Ficus hispida)

This is a very useful tree for the Khasis. They take this tree in a high esteem and many villages prohibit cutting down this tree. In village Nongjri there were many trees of this species which were used for collecting latex and export it outside for industrial use.

This tree, which gives out many roots from its branches and are very strong and long, the Khasis use to plant the trees on either side of a river and when they become matured with a number of roots hanging from their branches, they draw them from bank to bank and construct suspension bridges with branches and canes.

3. Ka Sangniah (Euphorbiaceae bridalia)

This tree is available in the plain areas and is very unique and useful as its timber is soft and can be given any delicate shape. It does not crack in the sun and wind. Khasi artisans use to make many useful household articles like spoons, forks, dishes, combs, musical instruments and decorative works of art.

4. Ka Dieng Jakrai

This tree was used in the olden days by the Khasi artisans to make rice plates and other household articles with this timber. The fibres of this timber are said to be very smooth and do not break easily while cutting in delicate designs. Secondly, it has a natural brown colour and therefore requires no painting. Thirdly, it does not crack or break in the heat of the sun.

Superstitions, Taboos Pertaining to Trees and Timber

The Khasis believe in the existence of a forest spirit, *U 'suid bri* or *U 'suid khlaw*. The Khasi word '*Sang*' implies an interdiction either religious or social from doing any particular thing.[17] There are special taboos set aside with regard to the use of wood or timber. The following are some, which are held lightly today:

1. To build a house with resinous timber. Only the syiem family can use such timber.

2. To cut trees from a sacred forest.
3. To use more than one kind of timber in building the hearth.
4. Trees or branches of trees falling on our way may bring bad luck to either maternal or paternal kins.[18]

REFERENCES

1. Gurdon, P.R.T. 1975. *The Khasis*. Delhi: Cosmo Publications, p. 36
2. *Ibid.*, p. 30
3. Chaudhuri, Budhadeb and Maiti, Ashok Kumar. 1986. *Forest and Forest Development in India*. New Delhi: Inter India Publications, p. 85
4. Gurdon, P.R.T. 1975. *The Khasis*. Delhi: Cosmo Publications, p. 32
5. *Ibid.*, p. 37
6. Lyngdoh, Mary Priscilla Rina. 1991. *The Festivals in the History and Culture of the Khasi*. New Delhi: Vikas Publishing House, p. 74
7. Gurdon, P.R.T. 1975. *The Khasis*. Delhi: Cosmo Publications, p. 39
8. Khongsit, S. 1999. *Kiba Ngi Khot Ja*. Shillong : Mrs. Sucila Khongngain, SanMer, p. 17
9. Gurdon, P.R.T. 1975. *The Khasis*. Delhi: Cosmo Publications, p. 23
10. *Ibid.*, p. 25
11. Mawrie, H.O. 1972. *Ka Pyrkhat U Khasi*. Nongkrem: Kong Tmissilda, p. 84
12. Bareh, Hamlet. 1985. *The history and culture of the khasi people*. Guwahati : Spectrum Publications, p. 427
13. *Ibid.*, p. 428
14. Tiwari, B.K. *et al*. 1999. "Sacred Forests of Meghalaya", Regional Centre, National Afforestation and Eco-Development Board, NEHU, Shillong, p. 14.
15. *Ibid.*, pp. 13-14
16. *Ibid.*, p. 14
17. Gurdon, P.R.T. 1975. *The Khasis*. Delhi: Cosmo Publications. p. 158
18. Mawrie, H.O. 1972. *Ka Pyrkhat U Khasi*. Nongkrem: Kong Tmissilda Soh. p. 86

4 CONCLUSION

The forest occupies a central place in the socio-cultural and economic life of the Khasis. Ever since the time when they were hunter-*cum*-gatherers they have maintained a deep symbiotic relationship with the natural environment which has played a dominant role in determining the history of their socio-cultural life. The indelible mark that the forest has left on the pattern of Khasi thinking and behaviour, is visible today in their culture, customs and legends. The forest and every part of its natural produces are permeated into the sanctum-sanctorum of the Khasi religious rites, rituals and social ceremonies besides being useful in their daily needs.

The indigenous system of folk medicine made out of plants and herbs which is prevalent among the Khasis accounts for the rich ecological heritage of the Khasis. This ethno-medical knowledge that the Khasis have developed over the centuries has continued to serve the Khasi community even to this day. According to a research conducted by Biodiversity Cell of North Eastern Hill University, Shillong, the total volume of medicinal plants or their products used or consumed per year was 80 to 120 tonnes involving approximately Rs.2.5 crores per annum only within three districts of Khasi and Jaintia Hills. With the increase in the market value of medicinal plants and growing demand for it, hidden trading in medicinal herbs has become of lucrative business for many unscrupulous traders. This has caused a growing concern among local practitioners and environmentally conscious citizens for the rapid rate of species depletion. There is a lurking danger of some of the rare species of plants and herbs becoming extinct if this bio-piracy is not stopped by the government immediately.

Another remarkable feature of the forest resources of Khasi Hills is its rich floristic variety found in the sacred groves. These groves are home to some very rare species like ***Nymphaea Pygmea*** (found only in South Siberia and North China), ***Magnolia Lamugimosa*** (found in Nepal) and ***Hemalium Schleichii*** (grown in Myanmar) which add to the diversity of species composition in this region. A careful survey of the vegetation, however, reveals some alarming facts of gradual degeneration and extinction of some very rare varieties of orchids and plants due to protracted botanical exploitation. One such variety which is facing extinction is Ilek Khasiana, a small evergreen tree that grows with thick foliage in the forests of Meghalaya. A great number of orchids and various species of flowering plants are brought to the local market for open sale by some Khasi villagers everyday. The law enforcement staff of the State Government or the District Council which looks after the management of major areas of the forest in Meghalaya do not seem to take due cognizance of the unauthorized floral exploitation.

Over the past few decades a tremendous change in the pattern of economic pursuit of the Khasis has been causing a great ecological threat. Economic development, pressure of increased population, industrial growth and urbanization has put on a combined felling of trees and denudation of forests. In the wake of the state-hood of Meghalaya in 1972, rapid infrastructure development, construction of roads connecting hitherto inaccessible and interior villages further paved the way for exploitation of forest resources in the state. Timber operation increased to meet the accelerated demand for timber for development purposes like construction of buildings and bridges, rural electrification etc. The mushroom growth of forest based industries like saw mills, carpentry workshops, plywood and veneer factories in Meghalaya and setting up of paper mills in the neighbouring state of Assam resulted in increased demand for timber and bamboo. The hectic activities in exploitation of forest, bamboo and other natural resources that ensued to meet the growing demand, led to wanton and mindless destruction of forests. The inevitable consequences of this human assault on the natural storehouse of the Khasis wrought a severe jolt on the traditional life and ethos of the Khasi people. The first victim of this situation are the poor who lost their food, water and fuel. The forest products such as tubers, rhizome, succulent bamboo shoots, mushroom, fruits and vegetables were not only their traditional requirements but also sources of earning by selling them in the market. Thus bereft of their traditional means of livelihood the weaker section of the society became alienated from their age-old occupation.

The long term effect of the denudation of forest was directly reflected on the ecological imbalance leading to climatic change, loss of bio-diversity and decline in rainfall which the people of Khasi Hills are presently experiencing. The temperature of Shillong during December-January (mid-winter) has never plummeted below 2 degree celsius during the last couple of years and the rainfall has significantly decreased lending to less volume of water accumulated in the Umiam Reservoir threatening the very sustainability of the Hydro-Electric Project. During the last two years the level of water in the Umiam Reservoir has dangerously dropped below the required level forcing the Meghalaya State Electricity authorities to resort to loadshedding for more than a quarter of the years (i.e. during dry season). According to some scientists the reason leading to this situation is due to lowering of water intake capacity of the reservoir as a result of heavy siltation of its bed which commonly happens in hilly regions. It is about time that the danger signal sent by nature is duly heeded by planned measures to reverse the trend at the earliest.

In the area of ecological conservation, a matter of some satisfaction is that the Khasis are still trailing the legacy of ecological knowledge given to them by their forefathers. Almost every Khasi village has a plot of green grove known by different names according to their use such as Law Shnong, Law Lyngdoh, Law Niam etc. These village forest groves are grown, preserved and maintained by every village primarily for three purposes—(1) For the use of timber during an emergency required by the village community as a whole or by an individual family. (2) As an abode of God or spirit to worship them periodically, and (3) As a watershed for supply of drinking water to the village. The Lawkyntang or sacred groves are preserved exclusively for worshipping God or supernatural spirits. The Khasis believe that both good and evil spirits dwell in the dark and gloomy forests, which are undisturbed by human beings while periodical worship and appeasement of these spirits would bring good harvests, peace and prosperity to the village and protect the inhabitants from famine, diseases and pestilence. These sacred groves are held in high esteem and sacrosanct. Not a branch of the tree shall be cut, nor a stone or grass-blade be removed from them. Violation of these sacred norms would result in a curse by the forest deity or 'U Ryngkew U Basa'. At regular intervals the villagers gather round the sacred groves while their priest 'Lyngdoh' performs rituals with offerings of foul and goats to appease the spirit.

This supernatural connotation of forest has occupied an important place in Khasi legends, folktales and literature. The forests or 'Ki Khlaw ki btap' as the Khasis call them, has since time immemorial endeared as a revered entity. Looking closely at the value system of the Khasi, one finds that it is centred on the supreme being (U Blei Nongbuh Nongthaw) as well as the transmigration of the soul and religious doctrines, which govern the family and social life of the Khasis.

Some anthropologists are of the opinion that sacred groves in Meghalaya originated not for preservation of bio-diversity but purely on the ground of threat perception of the Khasis that without the appeasement of forest spirits they might be visited by disease and pestilence. The supernatural protection against adversities may well be one of the intentions of the Khasi ancestors but the significant relevance that the sacred groves bear to the present environmental context cannot be overlooked. The rustic Khasi villagers of yore may not understand the concept of bio-diversity in the sense we do today but they had certainly the crude knowledge that the forests conserve water. This is evident from the fact that the Khasis keep dark forest groves around their sources of water from where women folk draw drinking water. Had this ecological wisdom not been there with the Khasis, many water sources would have gone dry by now in the present context of climatic change.

The ecological wisdom that the Khasis have gathered is the result of their age-long symbiotic relations with environment and their keen observation of various forms of nature and behaviour. It is the wisdom that is solidly based on experience casually derived in the process of their daily interface with the natural, forces around them while hunting-fishing, cultivating fields, gathering food etc. It is said that in olden times a Khasi killed a deer in the forest and he packed the deer meat in a few leaves of a plant. After the day's work was over he carried the packed meat to his home only to be surprised that the pieces of meat had turned to a single lump of flesh. This simple incident stirred his mind leading to the discovery of the potential property of the plant leaves in healing cuts or broken limb of a person. It is a fact that the Khasi indigenous herbal treatment of fractured bone is highly effective and has earned the commendation of even allopathic doctors.

The Khasis are dependent on forest and environment not only for their economic needs but more importantly they have a strong cultural link with the forest established by their ancestors. Ever since the days of primitive civilization when human interference on nature was the least and technology was virtually unknown, forest played its fullest role on the life of the Khasis. The numerous elements of environment in which they lived for ages moulded their culture, customs and behaviours. The indelible mark that the forest had left on the Khasi thought, belief and attitude can clearly be seen today in their culture, faith and religion. Their concept about God and evil spirits, their folktales and legends, their literature and poems, dance and music all are centred around the forests, rivers, streams, rocks, hills and valleys. Forest continues to be intimately connected to the life and economy of the Khasis till recent times and it has continued to play its multidimensional use in their life.

APPENDIX-I

LIST OF PLANTS AND HERBS WHICH BEGIN WITH THE PREFIX '*JA*'

1. *Jakhria* (*Rhynchotechum ellipticum*)
2. *Jalyngiar* (*Sunchus arvensis*)
3. *Jabuit* (*Acanthaccae; Phlo goganthus gamflei*)
4. *Jalyngkthem saw*
5. *Jalyngab lieh* (*Astecaceae; Senecio densiflorus*)
6. *Jalyngnap iong* (*Asteracaea; Inula cappa*)
7. *Jaskei*
8. *Jamiaw*
9. *Jamiaw madan*
10. *Jathang*
11. *Jatira*
12. *Jada dieng*
13. *Jada hati*
14. *Jada shnong*
15. *Jathynrait rilum*
16. *Jathynrait riwar*
17. *Jasnian*
18. *Jatung*
19. *Jarasong*
20. *Jalynsiang*
21. *Jatangniang*
22. *Jarain*
23. *Jakhain* (*Asteracsae; Pieris hieraciodes*)
24. *Jakhain pakhama* (*Asteraceae Hypocharis*)
25. *Jarem*
26. *Jarem saw*
27. *Jarem Shrieh*
28. *Jahynwet*

29. *Jaralud*
30. *Jali*
31. *Jali Sniang*
32. *Jali Krem*
33. *Jali Pnar*
34. *Jalynteng*
35. *Jalwain iong*
36. *Japri*
37. *Jasniang*
38. *Jalyngiem*
39. *Jawer*
40. *Janailar*
41. *Janailar Phud*
42. *Jalu*
43. *Jarumshiah* (*Zehneri heterophylla*)
44. *Jashun* (*Verbanaceae ruvella*)
45. *Jahynlaw* (*Viburnum cariaceum*)
46. *Jaiur*
47. *Jaiur jhur*
48. *Jaiur khlam*
49. *Jalynnoh*
50. *Jalynnoh skei*
51. *Jadaw*
52. *Jalyngbien*
53. *Japung*
54. *Japung ktieh*
55. *Jaler*
56. *Jalmut*
57. *Jalmut shniuh*
58. *Jamynsleh*
59. *Jamyrwai*
60. *Ka Jamynrei*
61. *Jamyrwait rit sla*
62. *Jamynrei ritbian*
63. *Jajew skei*
64. *Jakrai*

65. *Jakrai Lum*
66. *Japongdung*
67. *Jalyniar prohsla*
68. *Jamyrdoh*
69. *Jangew*
70. *Jalkhan Lieh*
71. *Jalkhan iong*
72. *Jalkhan heh*
73. *Jalyngkhan*
74. *Jaltham*
75. *Jawieh raij*
76. *Jalieh dymmiew*
77. *Japu*
78. *Jakba*
79. *Jalong*
80. *Jamiyiang*
81. *Jamiyiang synrai* (*Ternstomoceae; Camellia sp. F. Theaceae*)
82. *Jashiah*
83. *Jaler lum*
84. *Jakhaw shoin*
85. *Jashun*
86. *Japri*
87. *Japri lum*
88. *Jajew shilliang*
89. *Jajew shyrtong syiar*
90. *Jajew saw*
91. *Jajer*
92. *Jawieh*
93. *Jawieh*
94. *Jaum*
95. *Jalynnoh skei*
96. *Jalbuit*
97. *Ja Dieng Janai*
98. *Jating*
99. *Japiur*
100. *Japiur iong*

101. *Jasat*
102. *Jakhi iong*
103. *Jakhi shniuh*
104. *Jakhi rit*
105. *Jakhi nuli*
106. *Jaiing*
107. *Jalyngap sohriewlong*
108. *Jalyngap shymprong*
109. *Jarsang*
110. *Jasar*
111. *Janei*
112. *Jaryndem*
113. *Japang (Probila denticulate)*

Source: S. Khongsit, 1999. *Kiba Ngi Khot Ja*, Shillong: Mrs. Sucila Khongngain, San Mer.

APPENDIX-II

LIST OF SPECIES OF BAMBOO THAT ARE LOCALLY GROWN IN THE KHASI HILLS

Sl. No.	*Local Names*	*Botanical Names*
1.	U Tangei	
2.	U Namlong	Chimonobambusa khasiana
3.	U Stew	
4.	U Stew Ïong	
5.	U Spit	
6.	U Sylli	Cephalo satchyum pallisium
7.	U Tmar	
8.	U Dongla	
9.	U Shlu	
10.	U Spar Khlaw	Bambusa grififithi
11.	U Spar Bah	
12.	U Spar Ïong	
13.	U Spar Lum	
14.	U Spar Naha	
15.	U Sba	
16.	U Sba Heh	
17.	U Siej Naka	Phylostechyus manü
18.	U Tyr-a Riwar	Cephalo stashyum cepitatum
19.	U Tyr-a Bhoi	Dendrodavanauios
20.	U Muri	
21.	U Rñai	
22.	U Rñai shilot	
23.	U Rñai Ïong	
24.	U Pautabat	
25.	U Rthem	
26.	U Sken	Dendocalamus hamiltonü
27.	U Shken Ïong	
28.	U Tanglar	
29.	U Tawang Ïong	
30.	U Siej Lieh	
31.	U Siej Saw	
32.	U Siej Ïong	

Sl. No.	*Local Names*	*Botanical Names*
33.	U Siej Buid	
34.	U Smit	
35.	U Tyrkhaw	
36.	U Naka Ĩong	
37.	U Jympun	
38.	U Stem	
39.	U Makar	
40.	U Latuba	
41.	U Siej Thohrew	
42.	U Siej Makar	
43.	U Siej Khongpong	

Source : S. Khongsits, 1999. *Hangne Tang Ĩa U Siej*, Shillong : Mrs. Sucila Khongngain San Mer.

BIBLIOGRAPHY

Allen, B.C. 1980. *Gazetteer of the Khasi and Jaintia Hills, Garo Hills, Lushai Hills*. New Delhi: Gian Publications.

Arnold, David. 1996. *The Problem of Nature*. UK : Blackwell Publishers.

Arnold, David and Guha, Ramchandra (eds.). 1996. *Nature, Culture, and Imperialism: Essays on the Environmental History of South Asia*. Delhi: Oxford University Press.

Bareh, Hamlet. 1985. *The History and Culture of the Khasi People*. Guwahati : Spectrum Publication.

Bareh, Hamlet. 2001. *The Economy of Meghalaya: Tradition to Transition*, Guwahati: Spectrum Publications.

Barpujari, H K. 1992. *The Comprehensive History of Assam* (Vols. III, IV and V) Guwahati: Spectrum Publications.

Centre for Science and Environment, 1985. 'The State of India's Environment 1984-85: A Second Citizen's Report'. New Delhi: Centre for Science and Environment.

Chaudhuri, Budhadeb and Maiti, Ashok Kumar. 1986. *Forest and Forest Development in India*. New Delhi: Inter India Publications.

Chaudhury, J.N. (1978). *The Khasi Canvas*. Shillong: Smt. Jaya Chaudhury.

Darlong, V.T. (2002) 'An Overview of Forest Policies and Legislations vis-à-vis Forest Resource Management in North-East India' in B. Datta Ray & K. Alam (ed.) *Forest Resources in North East India*. New Delhi : Omsons Publications.

Dutta, B.B. and Karna, M.N. (1987). *Land Relations in North East India*, New Delhi: People's Publishing House.

Evans, Julian. (2001). *The Forests Handbook*. (Vol. I). London: Blackwell Science Ltd.

FSI. (1989, 1997, 2001). 'The State of Forests Report 1989'. Dehradun: Forest Survey of India.

Gadgil, Madhav and Guha, Ramchandra. (1992). *This Fissured Land, An Ecological History of India*. Delhi: Oxford University Press.

Gopalakrishnan, R. (1995). *Meghalaya: Land and People*, New Delhi: Omsons Publications.

Government of Meghalaya. 'District Level Key Statistics, Meghalaya, 2001'. Shillong: Directorate of Economics and Statistics.

Government of Meghalaya. (1990-95). 'Eighth Five-Year Plan' (Vol. II) Shillong: Planning Department.

Government of Meghalaya. (2003). *Meghalaya: Socio-Economic Review*. Shillong: Directorate of Economics and Statistics.

Guha, Ramachandra. (1994). *Social Ecology*. New Delhi: Oxford University Press.

Gurdon, P.R.T. (1975). *The Khasis*. Delhi: Cosmo Publications.

Hardy, Thomas. (1920). *Under the Greenwood Tree*. London: Macmillan.

Khongphai, A.S. 1974. *Principles of Khasi Law*. Shillong : The Author.

Lyngdoh, Mary Priscilla Rina. (1991). *The Festivals in the History and Culture of the Khasi*. New Delhi: Vikas Publishing House.

Mathew, T. (1980). *Tribal Economy of North-Eastern Region*. Guwahati: Spectrum Publications.

Mathur, P.R.G. (1979). *Khasi of Meghalaya*. Delhi: Cosmo Publications.

Mawrie, H.O. (1979). "God and Man" in *Khasi Heritage*. Shillong: Seng Khasi.

Mawrie, H.O. (1981). *The Khasi Milieu*. New Delhi: Concept Publishing Company.

Mawrie, L. Barnes. 2001. *The Khasis and their Natural Environment*. Shillong: Vendrame Institute Publication.

Mawthoh, P.R. (1984). "The Environmental Problems of Meghalaya" in I.J.S. Jaswal (ed.), *Status of Ecology*, Punjab: Punjab Publishing House.

Mukherjee, Anita Roy. 1995. *Forest Resources Conservation and Regeneration: A Study of West Bengal Plateau*. New Delhi: Concept Publishing Company.

Nongbri, Tiplut. (2003). *Development, Ethnicity and Gender: Select Essays on Tribes in India*. New Delhi: Rawat Publications.

Nongkynrih, A.K. (2000). *Human Development in Khatar Shnong*. Shillong: F. Nongkynrih.

Phira, J.M. 1989. *The Meghalaya Land and Revenue Manual*. Shillong : Government of Meghalaya.

Rawat, Ajay S. (1991). *History of Forestry in India*. New Delhi: Indus Publishing Company.

Ray, B. Datta and Alam, K. (2002). *Forest Resources in North East India*. New Delhi: Omsons Publications.

Regional Centre for Social Forestry and Wastelands Development, (1991) *Survival of Trees in Social Forestry Plantations of Meghalaya*, NEHU, Shillong,

Roy, Hipshon. (1979). *Khasi Heritage*. Shillong: Seng Khasi.

Rymbai, R.T. (1980). "Some Aspects of the Religion of the Khasi-Pnars" in Sujata Miri (ed.). *Religion and Society of North East India*. New Delhi: Vikas Publishing House Ltd.

Rymbai, T. *et al*. (1974). "Report of the Land Reforms Commission", Government of Meghalaya, Shillong.

Sarma, Sidheswar. (2003). *Meghalaya the Land and Forest: A Remote Sensing Based Study*. Guwahati: Geophil Publishing House.

Semple, Ellen Churchill, (1911). Influence of Geographic Environment on the Basis of Ratzel's System of Anthro. Geography, London.

Simon, I.M. (1991). "Meghalaya District Gazetteers", Government of Meghalaya, Arts and Culture Department, Shillong.

Singh, Daman. (1996). "The Last Frontier – People and Forests in Mizoram", Tata Energy Research Institute, New Delhi.

Sinha, A.C. (1993). *Beyond the Trees, Tigers and Tribes: Historical Sociology of the Eastern Himalayan Forests*. New Delhi: Har Anand Publications.

Sinha, A.C. (1994). *North-Eastern Frontier of India*. New Delhi: Indus Publishing Company.

The United Khasi-Jaintia Hills Autonomous District (Management and Control of Forests) 1958, 1960 Acts and Rules, 1995. Shillong: Khasi Hills Autonomous District Council.

Tiwari, B.K. and Singh Surendra. (1995). *Ecorestoration of Degraded Hills*. Shillong: Kaushal Publications.

Tiwari, B.K. *et al*. (1999). "Sacred Forests of Meghalaya", Regional Centre, National Afforestation and Eco-Development Board, NEHU, Shillong.

Uberoi, Patricia. (ed). 1993. *Family, Kinship and Marriage in India*. Delhi : Oxford University Press.

Vidyarthi, L.P. and Rai, B.K. (1976). *Tribal Culture of India*. New Delhi: Concept Publishing Company.

Worster, D. (ed). 1998. *"The Ends of the Earth : Perspectives on Modern Environmental History"*, Cambridge.

Vernacular Publications

Khongsit, S. (1999). *Hangne TangÏa USiej*. Shillong: Mrs.Sucila Khongngain. San Mer.

Khongsit, S. (1999). *Kiba Ngi Khot Ja*. Shillong: Mrs.Sucila Khongngain, San Mer.

Khongsit, S. (2001). *Ki Khlaw Ki Btap bad Ki Kam Ri Ngap*. Shillong: Mrs. Sucila Khongngain, San Mer.

Mawrie, H.O. 1972. *Ka Pyrkhat U Khasi*. Nongkrem: Kong Tmissilda Soh.

——,(1990). *Ka Theology Jong Ka Niam Khasi*. Nongkrem: Kong Tmissilda Soh.

Ramsiej, K. Dhirendro. (1992). *Ka Mariang Ha U Khasi bad ki Purinam-Puriskam*. Shillong: Smti I. Mylliem Nongpathaw.

Index